STORYWORLD FIRST

Jill Williamson

STORYWORLD
FIRST

Creating a unique
fantasy world
for your novel

N
teen

Library of Congress Cataloging-in-Publication Data
An application to register this book for cataloging has been filed with the
Library of Congress.

The author is represented by MacGregor Literary Inc. of Hillsboro, OR.

Cover Design: Jill Williamson
Cover photos: illustrations by Virginia Frances Sterrett- public domain;
sketches © Brad and Jill Williamson; model photo © Jill Williamson
Cover model: Brooke Pereira
Interior Design: Jill Williamson

International Standard Book Number: 978-0-9887594-7-3

Printed in the United States of America

To the weird ones:
You are not alone.

TABLE OF CONTENTS

1. CREATING THE WORLD 1
2. CREATING A MAP 9
3. CREATING CIVILIZATIONS 15
4. CREATING CREATURES 25
5. CREATING MAGIC 39
6. CREATING HISTORY 51
7. CREATING GOVERNMENTS 55
8. CREATING RELIGIONS 61
9. CREATING TECHNOLOGY 67
10. CREATING LANGUAGES 77
11. VERNACULAR LANGUAGE 83
12. WORLDS WITHIN OUR WORLD 91
13. STORYWORLD BUILDER'S DISEASE 95
14. HOW TO KEEP TRACK OF IT ALL 99
15. INTEGRATING STORYWORLD 103
16. MY STORYWORLD 109
17. BONUS CHAPTER: WRITING WAR 115
EXTRAS
    SOLAR SYSTEM WORKSHEET 124
    CIVILIZATION WORKSHEET 125
    MAGIC WORKSHEET 126
    STORY PLOTTING CHARTS 127
    CHARACTER WORKSHEET 129
    CREATURE WORKSHEET 130
    HISTORY OF ER'RETS 131
    SAMPLE MAPS 135
    ANSWERS TO SLANG QUIZ FROM CHAPTER 11 140
    WORD LIST FOR NAMING FANTASY PLACES 141
    WORD LIST FOR NAMING SCIENCE FICTION PLACES 145
    WORD LIST FOR CURSES AND INSULTS 149
    EXAMPLES OF DOGGEREL 151
    WRITING CRAFT TERMS 153
    SPECULATIVE FICTION SUBGENRES 154
    BOOKS I RECOMMEND 159
    BIBLIOGRAPHY 160
    ACKNOWLEDGEMENTS 161

ABOUT THIS BOOK

Oz, Wonderland, Narnia, the 100 Acre Wood, Neverland, Hogwarts, the United Federation of Planets, Westeros, Middle Earth, Alagaesia, Terabithia, Gotham City, Jurassic Park, Fablehaven, and a galaxy far, far away.

These fictional places have become real in the minds and hearts of readers. These are storyworlds that someone invented—someone who was once like you, learning to tell stories, learning to write, and dreaming about publishing a novel.

You have the ability to create such a world for readers. Isn't that incredible?

If you're a beginner who's overwhelmed by the idea of creating an entire world or who's uncertain where to start, this book will help you.

But if you're looking for a book to magically give you the ability to create worlds without doing a lot of work, I'm sorry to be the bearer of bad news. Writing a book can be loads of fun, but it's not easy. And coming up with a unique storyworld to go along with your book can complicate the process even more.

Worlds are not created overnight. They take time, patience, practice, and persistence to build. Still, this is my favorite kind of work. If you want help with that—if you want to create a story that stands out from others—this book will provide tools to help.

There's no *one way* or *right way* to build a storyworld. I'm a builder by nature. (You can read my story in chapter 16.) So, I'm going to take you through my process in hopes that it will inspire you.

I'm a checklist girl. I make a list of the areas that need special attention, then do them one at a time. But I'm also creative, and I often choose to ignore certain things on my own lists.

Story is key. It trumps everything else.

I have an author friend who starts her brainstorming by making a collage. She'll tear through magazines and print images from the internet, and sometimes draw or paint to create a collage of the world she's going to create. And when she's done, it sits by her computer while she writes, a constant inspiration.

I tell you this to impress upon you the vast differences in storyworld creation styles, but also to stress to you that this book is not meant to be a "To Do" list. Writing good speculative fiction is about immersing your reader in the world you've created. No writer does that in the exact same way.

Few stories go in depth on every aspect of a storyworld, and trying to do everything in every book can drive you crazy and bog down your story. In this book I've given you the tools I use to create worlds, but you must decide how best to use them. Find your own process as a writer. Embrace your creativity and trust your instincts.

This book is all about creating a mythical storyworld, but you could apply these same principles in creating a contemporary place like Bedford Falls, New York.

It doesn't matter if you're starting from scratch or looking to add realism to a story you've already written. The topics in this book can be applied to all stages of the creative process.

So, hold on to your fezzes! It's going to be a wild ride.

CREATING THE WORLD

GENRE

The first thing you need to do when creating a storyworld is decide what kind of story you're going to tell. An epic fantasy novel requires a different level of worldbuilding compared to a heroic fantasy. And a middle grade science fiction story requires much less worldbuilding compared to an adult science fiction one.

So what do you have? Swords or blasters? Horses or land speeders? An urban or rural environment? For what age readers?

If you don't know what genre your story is, I suggest you read. When you've found some books that are pretty close to the type of story you're writing, note which genre they are sold in. If you still need help, skip ahead and look at the Speculative Fiction Subgenres article in the Extras section of this book.

If you're not sure which genre you want to write, go with your strengths. I've written some science fiction novels, but I'm no scientist. And the amount of research I have to do to write a believable science fiction novel is tough for me. It doesn't come easily, and that makes it harder for me to tell a good story. (Plus, I get grouchy when I'm writing them.)

I'm happiest writing fantasy. But it took me writing ten books to figure that out. Sometimes you have to try different genres to know what you like best. And that's okay.

RELEVANCE

In each area of worldbuilding, take into account the plot of the book you're writing. If the story centers on one family living in the mountains, you might not need to spend much time developing the inner-workings of the government for the region. But if your story takes place in a castle, the politics of court life in your world might require more of your attention.

Your characters and what's happening to them trumps storyworld. Always. Worldbuilding is cool and fun, but you must not get so caught up in it that you ruin your book. Writing is a balance of characters, plot, pacing, voice, and storyworld. Weave storyworld into your character's actions and dialogue, and remember that a good storyworld should complement the story, not take over. You want the reader to feel like he's there, but not like he's there on a tour.

So now it's time to dive in to some worldbuilding topics. Have fun with this, but remember to keep it relevant to the type of story you're telling.

ASTRONOMY

George R. R. Martin's *A Song of Ice and Fire* series has uneven seasons. The characters know that "Winter is coming," but how it all works is a mystery that the author chooses not to explain. In the movie *Pitch Black*, however, we get more information. Every twenty-two years, the planet experiences a month-long eclipse when all three suns go dark. And that's when the little creatures come out.

Think about the universe your story takes place in. Is it our universe in the present, past, or future? Or does your story happen in a fictional universe? Is yours an on-world story? Or are you writing about a spacefaring society that will require the creation of a solar system and planets?

Either way, take some time to think about the astronomical

characteristics of your world. It's unlikely that your planet would behave the same as earth does. Consider things like orbits, rotation, axial tilt, tides, habitable zones, the sun, moons, climate, weather. How long is a season? How long are your days, months, years? You can do some really interesting things with this. The level of information you give your readers can vary depending on the genre and your writing style.

GEOGRAPHY AND THE ENVIRONMENT

What does this place look like? I'm a visual person, so when I create a new storyworld, one of the very first things I do is draw a map of the world. (I'll talk more about maps in the next chapter.) To start, think about your story location. Is it a city? A region of land? A continent? An entire planet? Consider the terrain. Mountains, canyons, plains, and coastlines. Rivers, lakes, swamps, and oceans.

Do some research on biomes to find out what kinds of plants and animals thrive in what type of environment. Will your planet have multiple biomes: aquatic, desert, forest, grasslands, or tundra? Your planet doesn't have to be as diverse as earth, but it doesn't have to be a one-biome planet, either, like Hoth from *Star Wars* or Arrakis from *Dune*.

Pay attention to the plants and animals too. If you have a Hoth-like planet but your characters are eating tropical fruits, where did the fruit come from? Also watch out for everyday earth details sneaking in to your otherworldly story.

When you think about water, remember that rivers flow downhill into bigger bodies of water and eventually into the ocean. How might these things influence your plot? In *The Lord of the Rings*, the fellowship parted ways when they reached the waterfall on the river Anduin. The water forced them to take another path.

Study a map of Middle Earth. It has lots of interesting terrain like the Dead Marshes, the Gap of Rohan, Fanghorn Forest, and the mountains of Moria. Much of this geography comes into play in the story and adds depth.

What's the temperature like in your world? What's the weather like? Think about your astronomical factors and how they might affect the climate and weather.

What kinds of animals live in your land? Do you have any mythical creatures? Dragons? Unicorns? Something totally unique that you made up? I recently read the book *Dune*, and I was fascinated by the giant sandworms. But *Dune* wasn't the only story to use giant worms. The ones in the movie *Tremors* weren't quite as big and no one could ride them. Let's face it. Riding a sandworm is pretty awesome stuff.

If you're going to create your own animals, make them different enough from the animals we know. Don't have an animal called a gorse that looks like a horse and acts like a horse and pretty much is a horse. With speculative fiction, readers are already taking in a lot of new information. So make things easy on them. If there are horses in your world, call them horses.

Consider disease. Could something in your environment cause illnesses? A plant, animal, or something in the air? In *Artemis Fowl: the Atlantis Complex*, the Atlantis Complex is a psychological disease common in fairies who suffer from guilt. In the novel *Watership Down*, Myxomatosis is a disease that affects rabbits and causes blindness. In Stephen King's *The Stand*, most of earth's population was killed off by a superflu. And in my book *Captives*, the people in the Safe Lands all have the Thin Plague, which is central to the plot.

What about natural resources? In *Dune*, the planet Arrakis didn't have much water, but it had a lot of "spice," which was an addictive substance that gives the consumer telepathic abilities. In *The Empire Strikes Back*, the planet Bespin is rich in tibanna gas, which is refined and used to make blasters and coolant for starships.

These types of things can affect the plot in different ways. In *Dune*, the desert Fremen learn to recycle their body's water and the overuse of spice turns their eyes blue. In *The Empire Strikes Back*, Cloud City is rich because of the tibanna gas, which drew the interest of the empire to try and extort money, which was why Lando made the deal to hand over Han Solo. The trick isn't merely coming up with a lot of cool things, but in deciding how these things interact with your plot and characters, and how they come into conflict with other aspects of your storyworld. That's what makes things interesting.

CITIES & TOWNS

Originally, towns were formed around places that saw a lot of traffic like forts or castles; monasteries or cathedrals; crossroads or market crosses, where people came to trade goods; active bays; and fertile valleys. Cities also formed on defendable hilltops or near natural resources like a coal mine.

What kinds of cities and towns does your world have and how did they start? Consider some interesting cities like the planet Coruscant in *Star Wars*, where the entire planet is one big city; the Emerald City of Oz, which is green; Hamunaptra, the city of the dead, from the movie *The Mummy*, a fictional city in which Imhotep's priests were mummified alive; and Brandon Sanderson's *Elantris*, a city that was once magnificent and now is in ruins.

A NOTE ON DEMOGRAPHICS

When I create a world, I tend to choose a place and time in our world's history and research the number of people per square mile. That gives me a good idea of how many people live in my land. I can also research the average population of cities, towns, and villages, which allows me to figure out how many, if any, businesses might be found in different places. When figuring populations, keep in mind that the desert supports fewer people than fertile land. The more food and water, the more people.

When I was worldbuilding my *Blood of Kings* trilogy, I created a chart for each city. I used a set of encyclopedias to look up places on earth that I felt were similar. For example, the landscape and climate of Barth is similar to northern Africa. So I looked up some countries in northern Africa in the encyclopedias and jotted down climate, crops, animals, plants, industry—that sort of thing. The process helped me understand what it might be like to live in each of my cities.

I included a Civilization Worksheet in the Extras section of this book, but you can download a full-size copy from my website: www.jillwilliamson.com/teenage-authors/helps.

LANDMARKS & BUILDINGS

With earth's vast history, there have been many examples of iconic architecture throughout time. Consider the Seven Wonders of the Ancient Word or something as interesting as Stonehenge or Mount Rushmore. Our planet also has breathtaking landmarks like the Grand Canyon, the Great Lakes, or Victoria Falls.

Give your world some of that. It needs natural landmarks, and unique, manmade structures add character to a land.

In my *Blood of Kings* books, the Gadowl Wall was built to serve as a border between two cities that always fought. And the Memorial Tree is a half-living, half-dead tree underneath which the previous king and queen were murdered . . . the place where the curse of darkness began.

Think of the lamppost in the Narnia books, the Doctor's Tardis, the Hogwarts castle, the yellow brick road from Oz, the Daily Planet building from Superman with the giant globe on top, the USS Enterprise. Or what about the Gates of Argonath or Pillars of Kings from *The Lord of the Rings*, which are the two gigantic statues of Isildur and Anárion that stand on either side of the river Anduin. Pretty sweet, huh?

SUSPENSION OF DISBELIEF

Reading is an act of faith. Someone picks up a book and instantly trusts that the author is going to tell a decent story.

When writing science fiction or fantasy, you sometimes ask the reader to trust you further as you take him into another world. This makes it more difficult for the reader to relate and presents an opportunity to confuse him and shake that act of faith he brought with him into the story.

So, when writing, it's important to keep in mind the term

suspension of disbelief. This means that readers will give you the benefit of doubt when reading your story. They'll hold off on judging you for implausible things—and maybe even some confusing things at first—trusting you to have it all make sense at some point. But if you push this too far, if things become too far-fetched, you risk losing your reader.

This is on you. It's your job to portray a world with characters, creatures, magic, and situations with enough realism that readers will believe it possible, or suspend disbelief, and enjoy the tale.

So tread carefully. Don't give your reader a reason to mistrust your storytelling. Use science to make your inventions plausible. Give your reader familiar things to anchor him to reality along with your strange new ideas. Don't have scaly snakes in arctic environments—unless you can use science to show the reader how it could plausibly happen. Don't have characters on a fictional planet listening to Michael Jackson music—unless you intend to show how this mythical galaxy is connected to ours.

The reader is ready to trust you. Don't betray them.

WHAT IT FEELS LIKE

You can write amazing descriptions and still leave your readers uncertain of what your world is like.

I grew up in Alaska without any running water. In summer, for baths and washing dishes, we hauled five-gallon buckets of water from a nearby river that was always swarming with mosquitos. I was a tiny thing and can't tell you how many times my wheelbarrow tipped over, and I had to go back for more water.

Winters were beyond cold. Forty below at times. My eyelashes stuck together. My dad's mustache and beard frosted around his face. But we didn't have to haul water in the winter. We just filled a metal tub with snow and balanced it on top of the woodstove to warm for baths or dishes.

There are other details that remind me of my childhood home. The bitter stench of sitting inside the outhouse. The faded sheet my mom tacked up over the window to use as a curtain. The towel on the floor against the front door to block the draft in winter. The soft buzz of a mosquito I couldn't see but knew was hunting me. The smell of the fire pit as my dad grilled hotdogs. The sweet smell of wild roses. The taste of the raspberries from the bush by our driveway. The dirt under my fingernails from playing in the sand pit across the road. The smell of fresh-split firewood, and the mess it left on my clothes after hauling it inside. The smell of creosote when the chimney got bad. The little market we'd walk to in summer where my mom worked and would make us ice cream cones. The old turquoise trailer, and the red and black school/house bus parked behind our home that we played in as kids.

All these details of my Alaskan home give you a strong sense about the place about where I grew up. You're starting to get a feeling for what it would have been like to live there.

You need to create that feeling for your storyworld.

Take some time to consider your world thus far. Have you thought about all the areas mentioned in this chapter? Have you spent lots of time on one area but neglected another? Look at your plot. Is there an area of worldbuilding you're missing? Something you need to spend some more time on?

All these things can add interesting twists to your characters' backstory and motivations, and to your plot as well. The "what it feels like" details can help to fully immerse readers into your world.

And that's what you want.

> If you're starting to compile information and need
> help deciding how to keep track of everything,
> skip ahead and read chapter fourteen for ideas.

2 CREATING A MAP

Ever pick up a fantasy novel and flip to the front to see if there's a map?

I do. Every time.

When there's no map, I confess, I get a little grouchy.

I'm obsessed with fictional maps. I love looking at them, and once I come to love the story that takes place in that world, I'm even more enthralled.

So when I started to brainstorm my *Blood of Kings* trilogy, one of the first things I did was draw a map.

Now, you may not be an artist, and that's okay. Whether or not your map ever appears in the front of your book, sketching it out can still be a really helpful worldbuilding step. I've also found it useful to sketch out floor plans of primary locations from my books, like homes, facilities, or castles. Doing this has helped me visualize the layout of a place so I could better describe it.

> Here is a link to maps, floor plans,
> and sketches I've made for some of my projects:
> www.jillwilliamson.com/maps

Before you start drawing, think about your story to discern what kind of map you'll need. You might be writing a science fiction novel that takes place on a made-up planet, but if your characters remain in one city for the whole story, a city map might be more useful to you than a global one.

Is there more than one nation involved in your story? Do these nations share borders? Are they islands? Is one nation larger than the others? Where are they located on your planet? Are they above or below the equator? Near the poles? Knowing this can help you determine climates, resources, types of vehicles, flora and fauna, and political advantages one area might have over another.

Also, put a scale on your map to show proportionate distance. Consider how much space and resources are necessary for the population of your land and position your cities accordingly. A scale will also enable you to estimate how much time it takes your characters to travel from one place to another.

Look at other maps—fictional and earthly ones—to help you with the shapes of borders and locations of cities. One thing I noticed when looking at Robin Hobb's map of the Six Duchies was that it looks surprisingly similar to Alaska, upside down. An intriguing way to come up with a map, don't you think?

When I started brainstorming my *Blood of Kings* world, I knew (1) the western side of the land was shrouded in perpetual darkness, and (2) there existed, somewhere, a half living/half dead tree.

But that's all I had. And if I was going to make this place believable to readers—and myself—I needed to be able to see it. That meant drawing a detailed map.

So I took a blank sheet of copy paper and drew a craggy outline. It was a little too big and looked a lot like Africa, so I erased a bit to get a more unique shape. I added mountains, rivers, trees, a lake, roads, a stone wall, and some islands. Then I added a bunch of dots to indicate cities in locations I thought one might have cropped up. When I was done, I had about forty dots.

That seemed like *way* too many cities to name.

So I erased half of them.

Much better.

Then I shaded my half-darkness over the western side of the land and added my half living/half dead tree.

But I still needed to name all those dots.

NAMING PLACES

How do authors come up with names for places? There are lots of ways. Tolkien invented his own language. Some authors use a phone book to find interesting names. You could use a map of earth, pick a foreign country, and choose names of cities, rivers, or mountains that have a similar sound to them. (If you do this, look up the meaning of foreign words just in case you chose one that has an offensive translation.) I like to get on Google Maps and look at street names. The last time I did this, I zoomed in on London.

If you're working on a map of a city, rather than a map of an entire land mass, you might also need to name areas, buildings, and streets. Think about Manhattan, New York. There are areas named after notable people (The Lincoln Tunnel, FDR Drive), by trade/industry (the Garment District, the Financial District), for ethnicity (Chinatown, Little Italy, etc.), for geographical references (Upper East Side, Midtown, West Village), and for landmarks (World Trade Center, Two Bridges, Battery Park City).

There are also places named by acronyms. Chester Rapkin, an urban planner, first used the term SoHo in 1962 for the area **so**uth of **Ho**uston Street. This started a trend for nicknaming areas in the same way. Consider the following list:

- DUMBO (**D**own **U**nder the **M**anhattan **B**ridge **O**verpass)
- NoHo (**No**rth of **Ho**uston Street)
- Nolita (**No**rth of **Li**ttle **Ita**ly)
- NoMad (**No**rth of **Mad**ison Square Park)
- SoHa (**So**uth of **Ha**rlem)
- TriBeCa (**Tri**angle **Be**low **Ca**nal Street)

I used this idea to name a city in my *Safe Lands* dystopian storyworld. Cibelo is the **Ci**ty **Be**low the **Lo**wlands.

When I set about naming the cities for my *Blood of Kings* map, however, I didn't think of any of that. I kept coming back to J. K. Rowling. She used Latin for many of her character names and magic spells in the *Harry Potter* books. I thought that was clever, so I looked on my bookshelf. I had a French dictionary and a

Hebrew/Greek concordance. I thought Hebrew/Greek sounded more fantasy-like than French. (Have you ever heard people speaking Hebrew? It sounds a bit like Klingon.) And since my story had a Biblical allegory, I liked the idea of using Hebrew words.

So I went with it. For example, "allown" is Hebrew for "oak" or "tree." So I chose Allowntown for the name of the city where my half living/half dead tree is. "Er'rets" is Hebrew for "earth," the same word used in the Bible where it says: "In the beginning, God created the heavens and the *earth*." So I named my fantasy world Er'Rets.

Having hidden meanings in your name choices can be a lot of fun.

But I didn't want to name everything Hebrew because, frankly, it's really hard to pronounce. (To this day readers tell me they wish I would have included a pronunciation guide in the *Blood of Kings* books.) And I also felt like a storyworld should be more diverse than having one language.

To help me accomplish a small level of diversity in my cities, I gave each one a theme. Allowntown, for example, exists in an area with many orchards. So I wrote a list of types of apples: Gala, Pippin, Cortland, Concord, Crab, Ginger, Fuji, etc. When I needed a new character from Allowntown, I picked a name from the list.

Carmine is a city surrounded by vineyards, so I made a list of things having to do with wine: Rioja, Flint, Terra, Keuper, Pinot, Concord, Malbec, etc. For Berland I used Inupiat names. For Magos I used Gaelic names. For Zerah Rock, I used names of stars. For Nesos, I used Hawaiian names. For Walden's Watch, I chose names that sounded like things having to do with oceans: Riif, Gil, Shoal, Aljee, Coraline, etc.

I did this, briefly, for every town that would play a major role in the story.

MAPS CAN HELP YOU PLOT

When you spend time drawing a map and adding in details, you'll come up with plot ideas.

The locations of sea ports, borders, roads, resources, the

distance to travel from one place to another, and dangerous things like volcanoes, quicksand pits, or lairs for evil beasts—all of this can inspire interesting plot twists.

For example, if there are two cities close to the only road that leads out of a mountain pass, that might create discord between the two cities as they fight for access to the road.

I drew a stone wall on my map because I thought it looked cool. But when I started thinking about why the people might have built the wall, I came up with the history of the two cities that have fought each other for years. At one point, the kingdom on the east built the wall to discourage their enemy from attacking again.

Creating a map can help you focus on all the important details of your world and give you a better grasp of what it's like to live in these places. And it just might help you map out part of your plot, as well.

Jeff Gerke wrote a great blog post on map making. You can read it here: http://bit.ly/1oIuXX2. For those who are not artistic, Jeff also recommends www.profantasy.com for creating maps.

In the Extras section of this book, I added some of the maps I've made to help inspire you. And you can always Google maps from your favorite books to help get your creative juices flowing.

3 CREATING CIVILIZATIONS

Hobbits, trollocs, Klingons, Fremen, myrdral, Wookies, Time Lords, kinsmen, vampires, Borgs, Uruk-hai, squibs, Chandrian, Nazgul, Terminators, crowls, werewolves, muggles, bloodvoicers, Vulcans, elves, Extractors, mistwraiths, Reavers, Weeping Angels . . .

I could go on and on.

But a civilization is more than one people type. It's a culture or society from a specific place and time that includes whatever species and races lived there.

In our world's history, consider the various time periods and the civilizations within each: the Ancient Egyptians of the Bronze Age; the Romans, Greeks, and the various dynasties of Ancient China during the Iron Age; the Aztecs, Mayas, Incas, Turks, and Eastern and Western Christendom of the Middle Ages; the Western World, Eastern World, Intermediate Region, and Sub-Saharan Africa of Modernity; and now the emergence of a Postmodern society.

In each of these civilizations you will find differences in people's way of life, race and ethnicity, religion, language, technology, and government.

For fiction, this can be even broader if you have different species and magical abilities.

When I create a new type of people or being, I like to start with something generic. I'll make up a couple right now to show you what

15

I mean. Let's say that "Gitals" are humanoids that use telepathy to communicate. "Kilns" are dog-like creatures that walk on two legs and can talk to humans. And "swigs" are sentient, slug-like people that, when angry, stick to other species like leeches and suck the water from their bodies.

Eww.

But those simple definitions don't go far enough. If I want to make each of these beings realistic to my readers, I must learn even more about them. I must study them. But that also means I need to invent the material I'm looking to study.

I take this one step at a time. In this chapter I'll talk briefly about each aspect of a civilization that I think about when creating new people groups. Some of these aspects will be discussed in detail in their own chapters later on in this book.

CULTURE AND ECONOMICS

Think about the way of life for every being and creature in your story, and understand that they won't all be the same. Ask yourself some of these questions:

Do they live in separate family groups or in some other manner? In what types of structures do they live? Mud huts? Caves? Fancy houses? Spaceships? What are their homes made of, and where do they get the materials and money to build them?

How does the economy provide for the poor, the rich, and all the people in between? What are the natural resources? Coal? Gold? Sheep? Silk? Wheat? Fish? Cool resources you've made up? What kinds of things do the people make, and how do they make them?

What do they eat? Where does that food come from? Are they hunter-gather people? Do they have occupations? Are they paid for their work? Is there money in your world, or do people barter and trade goods, use some sort of futuristic credits, or have they done away with money altogether like in *Star Trek*?

In medieval Europe, for those people who were not royalty or the highest nobility, there were four primary castes of occupations: warriors (men who fought for their lords or king, usually paid for with taxes), workers (people who farmed or learned a trade that provided them with money or something to exchange), merchants (people who made money buying and selling products made by workers), and priests (men who led by the principles of their faith, and lived off the tithes of believers and used them to help the poor).

Ancient Japan had a similar breakdown of samurai, peasant, craftsman, and merchant. Are there such castes in your world?

Who owns the land? Can anyone own land or only certain people? Does someone impose taxes on the people, or is the society the kind that takes care of its own? Is there magic? If so, how does it affect the economy and the culture?

Are your people educated? If so, is it by an apprentice/master system or in a school? Can everyone learn or only certain people? Why? Do your people care about arts, manners, morality, or upholding any laws? If so, think up reasons for why they care about these things.

What about gender roles? Are women suppressed in some way? Are men or children? How and why? In *Mulan*, only men could go to war. But in *Starship Troopers*, everyone, male or female, had the right to enter the Federal Service and assume full citizenship.

A NOTE ON EUROPEAN FANTASY

Some say that the traditional, European-style fantasy stories are dying, and that readers want new types of stories. I don't think that's wholly true. There are readers who find comfort in traditional stories, and those readers buy a lot of books. And there are also more progressive readers who are looking for the new stuff. Those readers also buy a lot of books. So I say write what you love. And if you're not sure, it might be fun to seek out different models of society to base your world on beside the Eurocentric kind.

Also, consider the magic in your world, if you have it. It will likely create some unique types of industry or occupations. In my

Blood of Kings trilogy, since I had the magic of bloodvoicing, I created bloodvoice mediators. These were gifted men or women who sat in on trials to confirm whether or not a defendant or witness was speaking the truth.

Need more examples of fantasy occupations? In the movie *Equilibrium*, clerics arrest sense offenders for breaking the law. In the movie *Minority Report*, there are three mutated human precogs, who have the psychic ability to predict crimes for the PreCrime division of the police department. And how about the extractors from the movie *Inception*, who go in and steal people's dreams?

Understanding the way of life for each of your civilizations is one of the most important parts to building a realistic storyworld.

RACIAL AND ETHNIC GROUPS

It's important to create races and ethnic groups that go beyond one dimension and keep you from having a monoculture in your story. Each should have distinctive characteristics that set them apart from others like physical attributes, religions, languages, and ways of life. How might these people groups have naturally divided themselves? Because of a skill? A physical feature? Perhaps they had a star on their bellies like Dr. Seuss's *Sneetches*? Or maybe differing histories set them apart. They could be a majority or a minority. Or there might be magical abilities that set some apart from others.

Once you've listed some characteristics for your different races and ethnic groups, make sure to find conflicts between them. In the original *Star Trek* episode, *Let That Be Your Last Battlefield*, the crew of the Enterprise encounter Lokai and Bele, two men with faces that are half white and half black, only the colors appear reversed from each other, a fact which seems inconsequential to the crew, but is an irreconcilable racial hatred between the two alien men.

The point is to give each group their own beliefs, ways of life, and subjectivity. But also remember that even within the same culture, people never agree on everything. If you can add that diversity within each people group, it should be a big step in creating living, breathing characters.

HISTORY

To bring life to a fictional people, it helps to create a record of past events. It doesn't have to be long, but try to come up with several key events that shaped your civilization. This could include eras marked by technological discoveries like iron, guns, or electricity. It might also list rulers, wars, invasions, major changes in government, or shifting boundary lines between countries. How about major plagues that devastated entire populations? You could even create some philosophers or famous authors that your characters can quote.

Consider making another brief history for a different people group. What does each culture believe about where life came from? If the land was discovered by someone, when did that take place and who was the explorer? Did something happen that sparked a change as to how two people groups interacted, like America's Civil War or the fall of the Berlin Wall?

The point is to not only come up with a list of historical events, but carefully think through how each people group would have reacted to or been affected by them.

RELIGION

Does religion exist in your world? Is there more than one? Where did those religions come from? Do people worship based on observation? The sun gives light therefore they worship it? How about cataclysmic events like earthquakes, eclipses, meteorites, or volcanoes? Perhaps religion derived from ancient texts? Or maybe writings on the wall of a cave?

If there's magic in your world or beings that have magical abilities, it could be that regular folk think those people are gods.

Don't forget to add diverse opinions to each religion. As I said before, people like to disagree about things, especially religion. How might each religion be interpreted differently? Also, see if you can make multiple religions in your story clash with each other. You can also do this by having characters with different beliefs. Make sure you know what each of your characters believes and why.

TECHNOLOGY

There are four major types of technology to consider when creating a storyworld: communication, medicine, vehicles, and weapons/tools. Take time to consider the level of advancement within those four areas for each of the people groups in your storyworld.

The technology of each group doesn't have to be the same and probably shouldn't be. The English devastated the French in the Hundred Years' War by their effective use of the longbow. If the French had also perfected the longbow, things might have turned out very differently.

PHYSICAL AND MENTAL ATTRIBUTES

What do each of your people groups look like? Be careful not to go too foreign with this or make it so far-fetched that it's not believable. The reader needs to be able to understand the people and be able to relate to them in some way. Giving them six arms might be too much.

Humans are humans, but you could play around with physical attributes. Just be careful of clichés like pointed ears and vampire fangs.

Let's take another look at that list of beings I made up:

"Gitals" are humanoids that use telepathy to communicate. "Kilns" are dog-like creatures that walk on two legs and can talk to humans. And "swigs" are sentient, slug-like people that, when angry, stick to other species like leeches and suck the water from their bodies.

Maybe female swigs are brown and male swigs are black. Maybe kilns have opposable thumbs but also have retractable claws. And perhaps one can't tell a gital from a mute human because they don't look any differently.

Let's take the gital telepathy a bit further. In speech, there are dialects and patterns among different social classes. Why not explore what that might mean for telepathy?

Perhaps our dog-like kilns have canine instincts, a pack mentality, an alpha male. Maybe they have a heightened sense of smell. Or maybe we should forget comparing them to dogs at all. Most authors do the easy idea. That's not always wrong, but it might be more unique to spin this in a different way. We could give those canine attributes to our slug-like swigs. Let them have the pack mentality and heightened sense of smell. Then we could give the dog-like kilns different instincts. Maybe they're nomadic and they travel for mating like penguins.

We talked about how the mutated human precogs in *Minority Report* have the psychic ability to predict crimes. Precogs also have a hive mind.

One of my favorite fictional attributes is how the biology of a Time Lord allows them to regenerate when they're mortally wounded. What an awesome and unique physical trait.

So play around with this and see what interesting things you come up with to make your people groups unique.

MAGICAL ABILITIES

Not every story needs magic. And even if you have magic in your book, not every being or creature should be able to do that magic.

We will talk in-depth about magic in chapter five, but for now, think about what kind of magic exists in your civilization and how it affects way of life and the economy. If a wizard can zap food out of thin air and sell that food for less than the farmers, he puts those farmers out of business. So think about ways to balance the power magic brings to your world. *good point*

HOW IT ALL WORKS TOGETHER

What makes a storyworld great is how all these elements interact with one another. Set out to create points of conflict. Perhaps one people group discovers a major resource on the holy land of another people group. Now you have a conflict. If the first people go after than resource, they risk starting a war with the religious group.

In the movie *Pacific Rim*, humans created massive robots as a way to battle monstrous sea creatures that were destroying cities.

In my *Blood of Kings* trilogy, Achan learns that he has the ability to bloodvoice, which is a telepathic magic. But he doesn't know how to use it and his untrained voice is a continual beacon to the bad guys chasing him. Vrell, another character in that story, is also learning to bloodvoice, but she's afraid of Achan's power and worried that he will find out who she really is. So Vrell spends all her efforts shielding her mind. Here the magic comes into conflict with itself as two different people learn to use it.

Another storyworld element in that book is my setting. As Achan and Vrell learn to use their magic, they are traveling through pitch black Darkness, which makes everything more complicated.

In my book *Captives*, the rebels have to cut out SimTags from their hands to avoid being tracked on the government's grid. Mason is a doctor and is able to quickly remove SimTags from others. That makes him important to the rebellion in a special way. And when the rebels need to pass through gates or want to be seen on the grid, they have to wear dummy SimTags in their gloves. In this way the technology of SimTags adds multiple uses to my plot and characters.

TAKE YOUR TIME

Creating a world is a lot to think about. I don't recommend trying to do it all in one day—or even one week! I like to start with a simple overview. For example: The world in the *Blood of Kings* trilogy is medieval-like with no dragons or elves or orcs. Bloodvoicing is the major magic type. And there's a strange Darkness that is spreading over the land.

Knowing that much about your world, you can begin developing your plot and characters, and even start writing. Then when you get stuck and realize that you don't know enough about your world, you can take time to brainstorm as needed. But don't waste days and weeks planning cool types of technology if it has no place in your plot. Be wise with your time. Be strategic. Your goal is to write a book. You want to brainstorm what's important to the story so that your reader thinks you truly know it all. The goal is that the reader will become so immersed in your storyworld, he won't want to leave. Ever.

4 CREATING CREATURES

Ever read a book and come across a creature so strange you could barely understand it? What about a creature that was pretty much the same as something on earth but had a different name, like calling a horse a gorse?

Then there are authors who choose to write about the stereotypical creatures that have been so overused like the centaur, dragon, fairy, ghost, griffon, harpy, manticore, minotaur, pegasus, phoenix, satyr, unicorn, vampire, werewolf, zombie, or even giant versions of cats, dogs, birds, or spiders.

None of the above are wrong. But the first choice usually means that the author is trying too hard to be original. The second two options often means the author isn't trying hard enough.

The point of this book is to help you create a unique storyworld, so let's talk about how to invent your own creatures that are both awesome and believable.

WHY DO YOU NEED THEM?

Besides trying to be unique, what's the reason for creating these new animals for your story? You might say, "Because I wanted some cool animals." And that's okay. But if you set your mind to it, you can come up with some reasons for fantasy creatures that will not only add to your setting, it can help your plot too.

Perhaps the animal is a pet, like in *Old Yeller* or *Winn-Dixie*. Or it could be helpful, like messenger pigeons or animals trained to work farms or pull wagons into mines. In *Eragon*, Eragon and his dragon, Saphira, had to learn to fly as a team. In my new *Kinsman* book, one of my characters, who is blind, has a trained wild dune cat that leads her around like a guide dog.

Animals could also be trained to fight in battles. Or perhaps people could make money gambling off animals that have been trained to compete in fights or races.

Perhaps the animals are a source of food and are hunted. Or maybe they are domesticated animals raised as livestock, for their wool like sheep or llamas, or for something made up like their magical tail feathers.

You might create an animal simply to attack your hero. I added fire-breathing bears to my *Blood of Kings* trilogy inspired by the images of bears on medieval heraldic flags. But once they were a part of my storyworld, I knew one would attack my hero at some point in the series.

Maybe the animal stands against the hero in some other way. Perhaps it guards a portal or magical object like Fluffy the three-headed dog in *Harry Potter and the Sorcerer's Stone*. Or maybe the creature obeys the antagonist in attacking the hero, like Voldemort's snake Nagini.

There are endless ways you could work beasts into your story. Maybe they're subterranean worms like in *Dune*, and some humans have learned to ride them. Or perhaps your hero needs something that only an animal can give, like the stag in Leigh Bardugo's *Shadow and Bone*. They could have a disease or venom that, when biting humans, could kill the person or pass on some magical effect. Maybe your animals are humanoid and talk and wear clothing, like some of those in C. S. Lewis's *Narnia* books. Or they could simply be an awe-inspiring (or fear-inspiring) part of the landscape, like the grazing brachiosaurus in *Jurassic Park* or the scuttling shadows and glowing eyes of the spiders in Mirkwood Forest in *The Hobbit*.

The point is to find a purpose for the creatures—maybe more

than one purpose—and integrate that into your story.

WHAT DO THEY LOOK LIKE?

Part of the fun of creating mythical beasts is deciding what they look like. I included a Creature Creation Guide at the end of this chapter to help you brainstorm all the details of your new animal's appearance. But don't forget your reader's suspension of disbelief. They're trusting you not to leave them lost and confused or to break the laws of plausibility.

That's why when I write a fantasy story, I never change all the animals. I'm already creating a made-up world that the reader must come to understand, oftentimes with a complex magic system. So I like to make it easier on my reader by including many regular animals like horses, dogs, cats, birds, etc. Then I'll invent a few of my own creatures to add coolness to the world.

The environment of each part of your world is important in helping you decide what types of animals live where. As I mentioned earlier, you wouldn't have snakes in the arctic because it would be illogical to the reader and pull him out of the story. So start with the environment when creating animals.

My new *Kinsman* series takes place in a desert land, so I started by researching what types of animals live in deserts. This gave me a lot of good ideas. I toyed around with replacing camels as the main animals ridden in the desert but decided that would be a mistake. And the more I researched camels, I was delighted to learn how unique they are. They quickly became fun minor characters in my story.

But I still wanted to create a variety of unique desert animals, so as I researched, I made a list of which types of animals most interested me. In the end, I came up with six: dune cats; some sort of cross between lizards, turtles, and saichanias; deadly, tick-like ants; a cross between whales and wooly mammoths; ossabey-like predator birds; and massive, lizard-like wolves. Then I spent some time Googling pictures of animals. I printed them out, and cut and taped them into versions of what my beasts might look like.

Another thing to help you decide how these animals will be perceived is to think about your main character crossing paths with one. What emotion comes over him? Fear? Awe? Disgust? Amazement? How do humans interact with these animals?

WHERE DO THEY LIVE?

We briefly considered the environment in which your animal lives, but let's take it even further. A habitat is the type of environment in which certain animals and plants live. There are three main types: terrestrial, which includes forests, grasslands, and deserts; freshwater, which includes rivers, lakes, ponds, bogs, swamps, and streams; and marine, which includes all saltwater bodies. One of these habitats is where your creature calls home.

But these are still broad categories, as I discovered while researching deserts for my book. There are many types of deserts. So I have an area of endless sand dunes like the Sahara, but there are also desert shrublands like in parts of Arizona, and high desert regions like in Eastern Oregon. Each of these areas are different enough that it affects which animals and plants thrive there.

Does your animal sleep? For how long? Do they sleep in the day or night? Some animals lie around all day. Some rarely sleep. Some hibernate in the winter. Where does your creature lay its shaggy head? Is it the same place it takes cover in bad weather or to hide from predators?

Wild animals live in a wide variety of places: burrows, trees, dens, caves, nests, hives, water, webs, and even under rocks or in rotting logs. Domestic animals live in houses, pens, and barns.

Some dog-like mammals live in packs, lions live in prides, grass-eating herbivores live in herds, ants live in colonies, bees live in swarms, and birds live in nests and travel in flocks. Many animals migrate to stay with the best climate and food sources. Some animals are territorial, keeping other animals away from the place in which they find food, mate, nest, or roost. Some animals live in a home range with many other animal types.

WHAT DO THEY EAT?

Three are three types of animals: herbivore, omnivore, and carnivore. Herbivores eat only plant material like foliage, grass, bark, flowers, algae, and fruits. Cattle, horses, deer, rabbits, beaver, koalas, geese, tortoises, elephants, giraffes, butterflies, and grasshoppers are all examples of herbivores. Most of these animals have flat teeth for grinding and small stomachs, so they tend to graze all day. Some herbivores gather food and store it for the winter.

Omnivores eat both animal and plant matter. Most humans are omnivores. The foods omnivorous animals eat varies. Bears will eat just about anything. They eat grass, berries, acorns, pine cones, mushrooms, roots, shoots, bulbs, insects, grubs, fish, crabs, clams, birds, bird eggs, carrion, and all manner of rodents. And if they're confident predators and hungry enough, they'll hunt deer, elk, moose, caribou, sheep, goats, antelope, bison, muskoxen, and wild boars. And if your story is contemporary, some bears are drawn toward landfills and trashcans too.

Other omnivores are pickier about their food choices. Chickens eat seeds and grains and worms. Orangutans are mostly foragers, eating whatever leaves, shoots, nuts, seeds, insects, and bird eggs they come across. Chimpanzees, however, are more aggressive and have been known to hunt smaller animals in packs and share the meat with each other.

Carnivores eat only meat by hunting or scavenging. Predators may hunt alone or in packs. Some are more calculating hunters than others—lions, hyenas, wolves, eagles, sharks, or polar bears. Then there are the smaller scavenging animals like raccoons, vultures, dogs, and crows.

So think about what your creature eats. Think about what, if anything, eats them. And if they are predators, know how they hunt.

DEFENSE MECHANISMS

How does your animal protect itself from danger? Speed is one of the most common ways for animals to evade predators. Many animals are able to camouflage with their surroundings. Turtles have a thick shell which helps them hide in their environment and also provides natural armor against predators.

Porcupines have quills, skunks have their smell, opossums play dead. Some animals travel in groups for protection, like herds of wildebeests or schools of fish. Packs hunt together to better bring down prey and to share the food with each other.

MATING AND DAILY LIFE

Some animals mate for a season, some for life, like many types of penguins. Some male animals have groups of females all to themselves. Some males fight each other over one female. Some female insects eat the male after mating.

Many egg-laying animals spend time building nests and watching until their young hatch. Male and female penguins take turns incubating their egg while the other looks for food. What kind of parent is your animal? Does it abandon its young or take care of it for a while?

What does your animal do all day? Many animals spend most of their time foraging or scavenging or hunting. Lizards sit in the sun to soak up heat so they'll keep warm at night. Some animals climb trees, some play (especially the younger ones), some go for a swim to cool off. Knowing these things might inspire a scene in which your protagonist happens upon your animal.

How does your animal respond to other animals or humans? Do they attack? Give chase to scare the intruder away? Growl and stay back? Run for cover? Completely ignore the visitor? Observe from a distance? Come when called? Or wander over on its own to say hello?

Does your animal have any special abilities? Think of some of the neat things earth animals are capable of. Roosters crow in the mornings. Monkeys and opossums can hang and swing from their tails. Dogs have acute senses and can be trained to track. Chameleons are able to camouflage themselves. Cattle have four stomach compartments and chew their cud as do sheep, deer, giraffes, and camels. Rabbits can see behind themselves without turning their heads. Owls can see in the dark. Bears hibernate. Mockingbirds can mimic any sound. Galapagos tortoises can live over 170 years.

Pretty amazing stuff. No animal can do all those things, but work hard to make each of your animals is unique.

PLANT LIFE

I briefly want to mention plant life. Most writers don't spent too much time creating a bunch of fantasy plants for their world, but it's common to see one or two unique plants per book.

Can you use any interesting plants in your world? What purpose might they have? You could come up with something to help your plot, or you might simply want to create plants that add beauty or uniqueness to your world, like massive ferns, reddish trees, or whistling reeds.

I created the âleh flower to mute magical ability in my *Blood of Kings* storyworld. In my current *Kinsman* series, I invented a desert water root plant, which has a celery-like root that draws water up from underground rivers.

Think about how other books have used plant life in their plots. In *The Fellowship of the Ring*, after Frodo was stabbed by a Morgul-blade at Weathertop, Strider tells Sam to find some athelas/kingsfoil to stop the poison. In *Harry Potter and the Goblet of Fire*, Harry uses gillyweed during the second task of the Triwizard Tournament to be able to breathe underwater. And in *The Hunger Games*, Katniss threatens to eat the poisonous berries, which is a huge plot point in the series.

So take some time to think about the flora in your world and see if you can come up with some neat ideas.

> ## A NOTE ON TRADITIONAL FANTASY CREATURES
>
> The point of creating your own creatures is to break away from stereotypes and do something new in your storytelling, something that's all you.
>
> But if you love traditional creatures, and that's what you want to write about, go for it. I want to encourage you to write what you love. But take what you know about these creatures and make it your own. Change one or two of the "facts" everyone knows about unicorns, dragons, etc. That way you can still write about them and give your readers something original and new in your story. Stretch yourself. Think

NAMING CREATURES

First, and most importantly, keep it simple. You want readers to be able to remember the name and be able to pronounce it.

The name should feel right. Don't name a beautiful bird a slithlop because slithlop sounds slimy and heavy and slow. Names can give readers hints about the creature. One would expect a timber gator would live in trees. You might also be able to give a name that fits the animal's personality or paints a picture in the reader's mind. Andrew Peterson is great at this with his bumpy digtoads, snickbuzzards, and toothy cows. Or you could combine animal types like Peterson's ratbadger.

Play with the obvious. Make a list of describing words for how your animal looks, sounds, or behaves. I did this with two creatures in my *Kinsman* project: the bluegem beetle; and lightworms, which glow like jellyfish. You could also combine description with an animal type, like furry pigs or red-beaked hawks.

Foreign languages can be an easy way to come up with names. I used Hebrew for many of my fantasy words in my *Blood of Kings* trilogy, and for some of the animals I simply looked up the word. If you use this approach, you might have to vary the spelling to make it easier to pronounce.

Be consistent with the tone of your world. It would be strange to use French names for creatures if you used Inupiat-style names for everything else in your story. Unless you're choosing names purposely to match different cultures.

Always Google any foreign or made up words just to make sure that the word doesn't have some strange or offensive meaning.

If you get stuck, you could try some of the online name generators. I've never used a name straight from a name generator, but I have played with them and been inspired. So it might be worth a peek if you're at your wits end.

CREATURE CREATION GUIDE

The following is a guide to help you come up with a new creature. For fun, you might sketch this animal as you read.

Consider each part of your creature's body and combine features that interest you and fit the needs of your storyworld, environment, and plot. Keep science in mind as you create so that your animals are plausible.

As we go, I'm going to use two of the creatures from my work in progress as examples for how to create an animal. To make life easier, I'll tell you their names now. The torterus and the drice.

SHAPE

Is your animal big or small? Fast or slow? Predator or prey? Domestic or wild? Warm or cold-blooded? Get a basic idea of the animal in your head by thinking of the needs in your story and what sounds cool. I thought it would be interesting to have a tortoise-like animal that was a predator. When it pulls its head and limbs into its shell, it looks like a craggy rock. Since my desert land is very hot, small animals might seek shade inside what appears to be small burrows. Then my creature would have lunch. That was the idea, anyway, and that gave me a basic animal shape to work from for my torterus.

Another idea I had was to have killer ant-like insects. I liked the idea that they would burrow into the skin like ticks, but they would be faster than ticks and eat their prey from the inside out. Kind of gross, I suppose. They mostly prey on small animals and wouldn't bother humans unless provoked. This idea was also enough to give my drice insects a basic shape.

SKIN

What kind of skin does your animal have? Is it smooth and slimy like a frog? Scaly like a snake, lizard, or fish? Is it covered in fur or hair? If so, is it thick or fine? Does it grow a winter coat and shed it come summer? If its body is covered in feathers, are they plain or brightly colored ones? Perhaps a hard shell protects the body. If so, is it like a turtle shell or a cockroach shell? Does your animal have a defense mechanism like porcupine quills or spines on a fish?

For my creatures, I knew I wanted the torterus to be similar to a turtle, but a predator. So I gave it a hard outer shell with a soft underbody that could slither out of the holes in the shell like a snake. Drice are so small, I didn't need to worry much about their skin, but I did make them sand-colored.

EYES

There are all kinds of eyes in the animal kingdom. Some see better than others. Some see at night. Some are large, some are tiny. I mentioned earlier that rabbits' eyes are positioned in such a way that enables them to see behind them without moving. Predator's eyes are right in the front of their face to make it easier to chase their prey. Subterranean animals have very tiny eyes or no eyes at all.

My torterus has round, golden-green eyes. There's a lot of wrinkly skin around its eyes so it can close them and keep out the dust. The drice has eyes that are so tiny you can't see them.

NOSE/SNOUT

What kind of nose does your animal have? A cute little kitten nose or a big bear nose? Or does it have a snout like a horse, cow, or crocodile? Does the nose do other things like smell or snort? If your animal is bird-like, maybe it has a beak instead of a nose. In that case, is it a tiny, pointed beak or a big, rounded one?

Sharks have holes that lead to a nasal passage coated with sensory cells that enable them to track blood. Elephants have that long, multipurpose trunk that enables them to breathe, smell, make noise, pick up food and eat it, scratch their eyes, and suck up water to give themselves a bath or squirt into their mouths to drink.

My torterus has two little holes for its nose. The drice are too small to worry about a nose.

MOUTH

For animals, the primary function of the mouth is to eat. The type of teeth an animal has depends on the size of the animal and whether it's a carnivore, omnivore, or herbivore.

Herbivores have flat teeth that are good for grinding food. Carnivores have sharp teeth for killing and tearing. They don't tend to chew much and mostly wolf down their food. Some predators swallow bites whole. Omnivores have sharp front teeth and flat back ones, sort of like human teeth. This enables them to bite and chew.

I talked about beaks back with noses, but beaks are also part of the mouth and are shaped to meet the eating needs of each bird. Carnivorous birds have sharp beaks that enable them to stab and grip and tear flesh. Wide beaks are great for scooping up fish or gulps of water.

Some mouths are very powerful and can clamp down on prey. Some mouths have fangs that may or may not be venomous. Some mouths have long tongues that can snap out and grab insects. Some have fat cheeks for carrying food. Some have no teeth. And some insects have no mouths at all!

Animal sounds usually come from the mouth or nose. Dog-like

animals howl, cats growl and hiss and purr, birds sing and cluck and squawk . . . What kinds of noises does your animal make?

Since my torterus is a carnivore, I couldn't give it a mouth like a tortoise, so I made it more like that of a crocodile.

The drice mouth is like a tick in that it has a center section lined with reverse spines that enable it to burrow into its victim.

HEAD

Is there anything distinctive on the head of your animal? Many mammals have horns or antlers to use for protection or to prove who's the strongest. Horns and antlers tend to grow with age. Moose antlers eventually fall off. Insects have antennae on their heads to act as sensors. Roosters and several other ground-feeding birds have combs on their heads.

EARS

What does the animal's ears look like? Floppy? Pointed? Round? Long? Or are its ears not visible, like with birds? Can it move its ears to become more alert, to hear better, or to show that it's upset or frightened?

HANDS

Does your animal have actual hands like a monkey or opossum, or paws like a bear or cat? Does it have claws? If so, are they short or long?

LEGS

Does the creature's legs have spines like a tick? Do they have multiple joints? Do they have suckers like a squid?

FEET

If your animal has feet, what do they look like? How many does it have? Two feet? Four? Or more? Do the feet look nearly the same as the hands, like a dog's paws? Do they have hooves like horses, or pads like a camel? Do the feet have claws or talons like an eagle?

TAIL

If your animal has a tail, is it long like a tiger's? Short and curly like a pig's? Able to open and close like a peacock's? A little nub like a hamster's? Bushy like a skunk's? Or various shapes like the tail of a fish?

WINGS

Does your animal have wings? Are they long enough so it can fly? Or are they short wings like on a chicken? Are the wings made of feathers? Are they leathery like bat wings? Film-and-veins like an insect? Do they flap slowly or so fast you can't see them?

FINS

If your animal is aquatic, does it have fins? How many? How big are they? Where are they located? Are they soft or hard? Do they have color or are they transparent?

Here are the final descriptions of my two creatures:

Torterus – A sly desert scavenger, this armored, lizard-like creature has claws and fangs. It roams deserts in search of weak animals to finish off or carrion to pull under its shell. It avoids open conflicts, but when it comes to a fight, this sharp-toothed shell-beast is hard to kill.

Drice – This tiny desert insect is almost invisible in the sand. They feed collectively on the flesh of other creatures by anchoring with their legs that are covered with hooked spines, burrowing under the skin, and eating their prey from the inside. Usually drice feed on smaller animals, but they have been known to eat larger creatures. When attacking, before they burrow, some take shortcuts through any orifice they can find—mouth, nose, ears. Some victims die of asphyxia when the drice crawl into their lungs.

 CREATING MAGIC

Magic is a tricky thing in fiction. Not all authors need or want magic in their books, and that's fine. But for those that do, it's important to spend time brainstoming that magic.

When creating magic, here are four important questions to ask yourself:

- What is the magic?
- Where does the magic come from?
- What are the rules for how the magic works?
- What are the limitations of this magic?

WHAT IS THE MAGIC?

Is this the ability to help plants grow faster? The ability to hear another person speak who is miles away? The ability to breathe under water? The ability to speak to the dead? Whatever it is, you must define it. See the end of this chapter for a list of different types of magic to get your imagination warmed up.

WHERE DOES THE MAGIC COME FROM?

Was your character born with this ability? Did he gain it by maturing in some way? During adolescence, perhaps? Maybe it came upon him through a mutation or evolution of some sort. It could have come as a gift from another person. Or maybe anyone can learn this magic with enough study and practice. Perhaps the magic is a language like in *A Name of the Wind* or *Eragon*? Maybe the magic is only possible in a certain place. Or perhaps the magic comes from an object like an amulet, talisman, grimoire, stone, wand, a piece of jewelry, a weapon, or a suit of armor.

Can anyone do this type of magic or only a select few? If everyone can do it, it's not as powerful as it would be if only a few are able. If only some can do the magic, why? What's special about them?

WHAT ARE THE RULES FOR THE MAGIC?

How does the magic work? Is it supernatural, does it come from nature, or can it be explained with science? Laws of nature make things possible or impossible on our planet. The same should be true of your storyworld. Think through how your magic is possible and come up with some rules. Without rules, you lose realism.

In my *Blood of Kings* trilogy, I created a magic called bloodvoicing. It's a telepathic magic that runs in one's blood, genetically, like blond hair or blue eyes. Bloodvoicers can speak to other bloodvoicers' minds, but they can also listen in on non-gifted individuals. Bloodvoicers can learn to fight with their gift as well, forcing a person's soul from their body.

It was this ability that forced me to create different laws of nature for my storyworld. I invented the Veil, a spiritual realm that bloodvoicers could travel in if they left their bodies. The Veil was the place between life and the afterlife, and so when someone was in the Veil, his soul was pulled in one of two directions: Shamayim or the Lowerworld.

The more you play and expand your magic, the better it gets. In an effort to make my magic different from plain-old telepathy, I played around with ways people might use or abuse the magic of bloodvoicing. Here is my list:

Messaging – Sending a thought to another person.

Listening – Eavesdropping on the thoughts of another with or without their consent.

Watching – Looking through the eyes of another while hearing their thoughts.

Knocking – The way to let a gifted person know you want to communicate.

Blocking – Closing your mind so that no one can send you a message or look through your eyes.

Sensing – Recognizing when a gifted bloodvoicer is nearby.

Jumping – Using another bloodvoicer's connection to reach a third individual. This is done in cases when an individual doesn't know their target well enough to make a connection on their own.

Influencing – Forcing someone to do something secretly or by outright possession. A naughty use of one's power.

Storming – Forcing someone's soul from their body and into the Veil.

WHAT ARE THE LIMITATIONS OF THE MAGIC?

Consider the source of your magic and how the characters harness it. Rumpelstiltskin, from the ABC show *Once Upon a Time*, often says, "Magic always comes with a price." If you create a price for magic, you'll increase the conflict and risk for your character, which creates conflict and makes the magic more believable.

Having a cost also keeps evil characters from taking over the world. But beware. There are many clichés in magical costs, like ageing or having the user grow weary with use. Try to come up with something unique and to balance the power and cost. If the power is small, the cost can be small, but if the power is massive, the cost should be massive.

IMPACT ON SOCIETY

Take all this one step further and think about how this affects the world. What are the ramifications of magic on society? How have the cultures adapted to the magic? How can the magic be used for evil? Can the magic be commercialized? Think about the magic's impact on farming, manufacturing, government, day-to-day living, and human relationships. How does the magic change those things? What things have come about as a result of those changes?

For example, if telepathy was possible for all people, we'd know what everyone was thinking. It would change the way people think, as they tried to keep their feelings private. You'd have to come up with new ways that people cheated others in business since they couldn't lie. Perhaps people could train themselves to think distracting thoughts while they spoke, to mask their lies. Someone might invent a helmet or potion that blocks mind reading. There might be laws against hate thoughts. If so, there will be lawbreakers who will be sentenced in some way for their crime.

There should also be different levels of skill in the magic, as well. In *The Lord of the Rings*, Galadriel has an extraordinary ability to peer into the minds of others, see their intentions, read their thoughts, and speak to them. Yet very few elves have this ability.

I gave my characters different levels of magical ability in my *Blood of Kings* books. Achan is powerful but untrained, so he often makes dangerous mistakes. Vrell is great at shielding but can't bloodvoice for long because it makes her weak—cliché, I know! Still, this puts her soul in danger of floating into the Veil if she uses her magic too long.

Once you've created your rules, stick to them. Your readers will know if you don't.

TRY AND FAIL

The magic you've created is new to your readers, so to help them understand the levels of difficulty, show your characters fail. Show their frustration and practice as they try to make sure that failure won't happen again. Yet, maybe it still does. This will help readers understand so much better than telling them the magic is difficult.

If your character tries to do something that is against the rules of the magic, write the consequences, which can be fun. For example, Achan was so powerful that every time he tried to "Listen" with his bloodvoice he ended up in another person's mind "Watching," which left his body empty and dazed—a bad move when his body was in the middle of a sword fight!

NAMING MAGIC SYSTEMS AND MAGICAL ACTS

Naming magic isn't all that different from naming places or creatures. As always, keep things simple and easy to pronounce. Remember to be consistent with the tone of your world and to Google any foreign or made up words to make sure they are safe.

Consider what we've already discussed:

- The name should feel right.
- Call it what it is. My bloodvoices did that since the magic is hereditary (runs in one's **blood**) and gives **voice** to one's mind.
- The name could hint at what the magic looks like or does.
- Name it after the first person to discover the magic.
- Name it from your made-up language, if you have one.
- Use foreign languages for inspiration.
- Use online name generators for inspiration.
- Name it after landmarks or regions where the magic originated.
- If a magical substance is used, you could name it after the place it's gathered, mined, or produced.
- Name it after an industry or trade, if there's one for the magic.
- Name it after a certain ethnic group, if they are the only ones able to do that magic.
- Come up with an acronym for what the magic does.
- Add a magic-like suffix to the end of your word. For example, add "light" to: −craft, −pathy, −nesis, −icry, −casting, −oyance, −emy, −ation, −mancy, −oning. ha

TYPES OF MAGIC

The following is a list of different types of fantasy magic or superhuman abilities that have become popular through ancient stories, novels, comic books, movies, or games. I'm no expert on this subject and have cobbled this list together through brainstorming with my husband and writing friends, looking things up in the dictionary, and by combing through the movies and books in my house.

It's not my intention that you pluck any magic or ability from this list and use it as it has been used before. My hope is that this list might inspire you toward something fresh in your own books. For example, the magic in my *Blood of Kings* books is a form of telepathy. But I took that that generic ability, combined it with my storyworld's "Veil" (a spiritual realm of sorts), and brainstormed ways that soldiers might use the magic to fight during times of war. After that, the magic took on a life of its own.

So take a look at this list. I tried to organize it, but it's still pretty complex. I hope it sparks some cool ideas.

Alchemy – The ability to change chemical elements from one substance to another, usually changing something of little value into something of great value.

Animation – The ability to bring inanimate objects to life.

Conjuring – The ability to conjure spirits.

Disintegration – The ability to disintegrate matter.

Elemental – The ability to control or manipulate the elements of nature (water, fire, wind, earth.)

Flight – The ability to fly.

Healing – The ability to heal oneself or others from injuries.

Illusion – The ability to create illusions.

Immortality – The ability to live forever.

Invisibility – The ability to make oneself invisible.

Invulnerability – To be invincible or immune to injury.

Mage, magician, sorcerer, wizard – A person who is skilled in magic.

Matter ingestion – The ability to consume any sort of matter without harm.

Medium – The ability to see and communicate with the dead.

Mimicry – The ability to mimic, absorb, or steal the abilities of people, plants, or animals and even another person's powers.

Necromancy – The ability to bring the dead to life and control them.

Omnipresent – The ability to be present everywhere at the same time.

Omniscient – The ability to have unlimited knowledge, awareness, or understanding.

Poison – The ability to poison another.

Possession – The ability to occupy, dominate, or control another person from within.

Scrying – The ability to use a magical item to view future events.

Self-detonation – The ability to explode one's body and reform.

Shamans – An intermediary between the natural and supernatural world. One who uses magic to cure illness, tell the future, control spiritual forces by using bones, totems, and sometimes by sharing an animal's senses.

Summoning – The ability to call for the presence of another, message them, or signal them by command. Most often involves demons or spirits from other realms.

Wall climbing – The ability to climb any surface, even vertical ones like Spiderman.

Water breathing – Ability to breathe under water.

Witchcraft – This varies. Fairytale witches and warlocks practice magic, especially black magic or black arts.

ABILITIES INVOLVING ENERGY

Absorption – The ability to absorb energy and convert it into something else, like physical strength.

Augmentation – The ability to enhance or weaken someone else's powers.

Bestowal – The ability to bestow powers on another or to bring one's latent powers to life.

Conversion – Ability to absorb one form of energy and convert it into another form of energy.

Electrical transportation – The ability to travel through electrical conduits such as: cell phones, computers, power lines, telephone lines, television sets, etc.

Energy manipulation – The ability to manipulate another person's powers into something else.

Force field generation – Ability to project powerful fields of manipulated energy that often act as shields.

Negation – The ability to mute the powers of another person.

Sensing – The ability to sense or recognize magical powers.

Sourcing – The ability to draw power from energy sources.

ABILITIES INVOLVING INTELLIGENCE

Intelligence – Being a genius, sometimes having the ability to learn new things quickly.

Linguist, polyglot – The ability to understand any language.

Probability – The ability to predict future possibilities, or to alter or change future outcomes.

ABILITIES THAT MANIPULATE PHYSICAL THINGS

Biology, metamorphosis – The ability to manipulate any aspect of biology: limbs, bones, hair, gender. One could change their size, make their bones stab out like spears, stretch their body, or change arms into legs.

Duplication – The ability to create physical duplicates of oneself.

Gravity – The ability to manipulate gravity.

Light – The ability to create, manipulate, or absorb particles of light.

Magnetism – The ability to generate, control, or manipulate metal or magnetic fields.

Mass – The ability to increase or decrease mass in an object or person.

Merge – The ability to merge two beings into one.

Quantum tunneling – The ability to travel through solid matter without harm, walking through a wall, for example.

Regeneration – The ability to regenerate.

Shapeshifting – The ability to assume a different physical form. There are many different types of shapeshifting. One could take on the form of an animal or plant, turn to liquid or gas, or turn into the substance they are touching.

Technopath – The ability to manipulate technology.

ABILITIES INVOLVING PSIONICS

Abuse – The ability to enter another mind and cause pain, loss of consciousness, and eventually death.

Empathy – The ability to read or sense another person's emotions and/or control another person's emotions or feelings.

Foresight – The ability to look into the past, present, or future.

Memory manipulation – The ability to erase or change the memories of another person.

Mind control – The ability to control another person's actions or reasoning.

Psychic, precognition, prophecy, clairvoyance (clear seeing), clairaudience (clear hearing) – The ability to perceive the future. This could happen in dreams during sleep or visions while awake.

Psychometry – The ability to gain foresight by touching objects.

Telekinesis – The ability to control, manipulate, or move objects with the mind.

Telepathy – The ability to read another person's thoughts or communicate telepathically with another person.

ABILITIES INVOLVING SOUND

Sonar sense – The ability to use sound waves to locate items.

Sonic scream – The ability to make sounds that are in higher amplitudes than the human voice.

Sound manipulation – The ability to manipulate sound waves.

SUPERHUMAN ABILITIES

Durability – The ability to have a higher resistance to injury than a normal person.

Reflexes – The ability to react faster than a normal person.

Senses – Having magnified abilities to see, hear, feel, smell, and/or taste.

Speed – The ability to move faster than a normal person.

Strength – The ability to have more strength than a normal person.

Vision – The ability to have power though one's vision, which could include heat vision, magnified vision, night vision, and/or x-ray vision.

ABILITIES INVOLVING TIME

Time mages – The ability to slow, accelerate, reverse, and/or stop time.

Time travel – The ability to travel back and forth through time or to manipulate time.

ABILITIES INVOLVING TRANSPORTATION

Dimensional transportation – The ability to create portals or wormholes between places.

Teleportation – The ability to move from one place to another instantly without actually traveling over the space between.

HOW MANY TYPES OF MAGIC?

I meet authors who excitedly tell me all about the multiple types of magic in their story. I usually lose interest after they explain the first one. Please consider the "less is more" principle when it comes to magic. Trying to do too many things weakens your story. It's much more engaging to have one complex and well-thought-out magic system than it is to have eight. One would make it easier for you to immerse the magic into every aspect of society, whereas having so many would erase the coolness and overcomplicate things.

The more you know about your magic and how it affects everything in your world, the better you'll be able to write about it. So take the time to come up with something unique and different and deep. You'll be glad you did.

6 CREATING HISTORY

There's much to learn about worldbuilding from earth's history. Civilizations rose and fell, and new ones cropped up. There have been extinctions, inventions, changes of regime, plagues, and wars. Oftentimes the strongest side won, but not always. Many rulers made mistakes that cost them the lives of their army and their throne.

Our world has a fascinating history. So should yours. It should not always be logical. It should not have the same rulers who ruled a millennium ago. But it should shape the current storyworld.

Be careful not to go too far with inventing history. Have a purpose for history. What conflicts are you setting up? You only need enough to help you tell your story. Also, don't slip huge sections of history into your book or have an information dump prologue. It's best to work in your history as you tell the story.

The history of English magic is used wonderfully in *Jonathan Strange & Mr. Norrell* by Susanna Clarke, and J. K. Rowling makes excellent use of the history of the wizarding world in the Harry Potter books, giving the reader information on a need-to-know basis.

CREATE A TIMELINE

When I started my first fantasy novel, I didn't know how to go about creating a history. I wanted to make it simple, so I wrote a timeline of my land. Really, it's a timeline of only one group of people, starting when they arrived in the land and ending at the time when my book began.

I started with the year zero, when the first king came to the land on a ship, and I went up to the year 585, when my main character would turn sixteen. I used Microsoft Word and typed a number and a hyphen for every ten years in a long, long line. Then I added to my timeline which kings ruled when, important births and deaths, wars, exploration and discoveries, when certain cities or landmarks were built—anything I thought might be worth remembering.

All this gave my land character. For example, I knew why the people from Cherem hated the people from Magos. They'd been battling for years. If a Cheremite and a Magosian were to meet in my book, it might get ugly.

And ugly is good because ugly means conflict.

WRITE IT OUT

I highly recommend writing out a history of your land. Go back as far as you want. For inspiration, Google the history of our world. Look at the different eras and see how we've advanced over the years.

I wrote a historical narrative for the land of Er'Rets from my *Blood of Kings* trilogy and little blurbs on each city. I did this for my own knowledge so that I could better understand the world my characters lived in. You can read *A History of Er'Rets* in the Extras section of this book. Keep in mind, I wrote it for me, so it's not perfect. And if you click on the link under the map after the history, it will take you to an online version of the map where you can click on different cities and read about them. This was all pre-writing I did while building my storyworld. None of this went in my book as is. It was for me to know so that I could better understand the world my characters lived in. I hope this serves as an illustration of what you could do and inspires some ideas for your own worldbuilding.

Don't spend forever on this! A little goes a long way, and you can always stop writing and create more history if needed. Remember, you're writing a novel, not a history textbook. Only take this as far as you need to. Then stop and get back to writing.

COMPLICATE THINGS

When you have different cultures, you have different ways of looking at things. How do other cultures remember the historical events differently? There's often more than one reason for a war. See if you can find ways to put conflict into your world's history.

DON'T USE IT?

That's right. Fight the urge to cut and paste whatever cool histories you may have written. Instead, tell your character's story. The history will come out if and when it needs to. Here are a few of the places I used my history in my *Blood of Kings* books:

•Achan learns early on that he's of Kinsman descent.

•Achan and Vrell meet giants, Poroo people, and wolves, all of which I created when I wrote my historical narrative.

•When Achan reaches the memorial tree in Allowntown, he thinks about the murder of the king and queen and the curse of darkness on the land, both of which are on my timeline.

•Throughout the book the reader is given different bits and pieces of the story of how the prince came to live with Lord Nathak.

•Characters talk about the Great War, which happened a long time ago.

I didn't use a lot of the history in the actual books, but without having written it, I wouldn't have had a foundation from which to create.

CURRENT-DAY CONFLICTS

Now that you've done all the hard work of building your storyworld, you need to get on with the story! And what is a story, anyway? It's a series of events designed to entertain your reader. A series of events that takes place in your fabulous world.

So, take a look at that world. What kinds of current-day conflicts have you already set up? Is there a threat to your world? A threat to a certain people? Is war brewing? Does your story's conflict involve the land in some way?

Here are some examples of how current-day conflicts from my books helped me establish my plots. In my *Blood of Kings* trilogy, Darkness is spreading. And that's a serious problem. In *Captives*, the people in the Safe Lands are dying from a virus, and they have to do something to save themselves. In *Replication*, Martyr just wants to see the sky before he expires, but Dr. Kane is also in serious trouble. His needs and Martyr's needs clash in a big way.

Let's also look at examples from other books. In *The Lord of the Rings*, Sauron has been looking for the One Ring for a while, and a hobbit just happened to put it on. In *The Lion, the Witch and the Wardrobe*, the White Witch has been doing bad things long before the Pevensies arrive, but she learns that children aren't as easy to control as animals. In *Harry Potter*, Lord Voldemort has been biding his time, building his strength, waiting to return. In *Cinder*, the political situation is not good. Emperor Kai must decide to marry the evil Queen or see his people die. What's a good emperor to do, anyway?

The conflicts in all of these books were set up by the history of the storyworld, long before the actual story began. That's what you want to achieve with your history. You want to set up your characters and your world so that your plot can happen.

7 CREATING GOVERNMENTS

Governments exercise direction and control over the citizens of their land. They organize laws and enforce them, and in doing so, maintain some sort of civilized society.

Government is not the same as politics. *Government* is "the institution whereby we translate public will into public policy, and *politics* is the process of government. The tension between these two is what makes *political science* interesting" (Lusco).

If you're creating a new world or a mythical one within our world, it's wise to spend some time thinking about how the government works.

This doesn't have to be complicated. But if you choose a type of government for your storyworld that you know nothing about, do some research to help you understand it.

Who controls the food and water in your storyworld? Who controls the weapons? If there's a disease, who controls the medicine? Whoever holds these things has power over everyone else. These people often make the laws, usually to their own political and/or financial advantage.

So, ask yourself who has the power in your world and why? What's the history there? If you're writing a book that has little to do with the government, maybe you don't need to go much further than that.

Also consider: How does the government restrict personal freedoms? Can both men and women live wherever they want? Can they work? Must they pay taxes? Must they pay for something else, like health insurance? Can they carry a weapon? How are laws made? Who enforces those laws?

If you want to write something different than the typical feudalistic monarchy of most fantasy novels or the intergalactic federation of many science fiction novels, consider using a different form of government.

Here is a list that is not at all comprehensive, but I hope that it might inspire some interesting ideas for your storyworld.

TYPES OF GOVERNMENTS

Anarchy – "A lack of formal government in which people are free to form voluntary associations from which they can enter and exist at will" (Lusco).

Aristocracy – A government ruled by the elite, privileged, upper class, nobility, or any group considered to be superior through education, ability, wealth, or social prestige.

Authoritarian – A government in which individual freedom is subordinate to the power or authority of the state and is not accountable to the people. Some types of authoritarian government do permit degrees of individual freedom.

Autocracy – A government in which one person (an autocrat) has uncontrolled or unlimited authority, power, or influence. Consider similar governments of despotism, dictatorship, stratocracy, fascism, and tyranny.

Capitalism – An economic system in which people invest in and own their own businesses and property. Wealth is made and maintained mostly by private individuals or corporations.

Communism – A classless society in which private ownership is abolished and the means of production and provisions for survival belong to the community.

Confederation – An economic and/or political union or alliance of sovereign states in which membership of each state is voluntary. Consider the European Union of today.

Democracy – A form of government in which the supreme power is vested in the people and exercised directly by them or by their elected agents under a free electoral system.

Empire – A group of nations or peoples ruled over by an emperor, empress, or other powerful sovereign, established usually through coercion.

Federation – A union of partially self-governing states or regions united by a federal government.

Feudalism – The political, military, and social system in the Middle Ages based on the holding of lands in fief or fee and on the resulting relations between lord and vassal. Under feudalism, the land in a kingdom belonged to the king, who gave some (called manors) to lords or nobles that served him. The lords or nobles gave some of their land (called fiefs) to vassals, who served the lords.

Libertarian – A government that advocates the freedom of thought, expression, and free will and protects its people from coercion and violence.

Monarchy – A form of government in which supreme authority is vested in a single and usually hereditary figure, such as a king. There are different types of monarchies to consider: absolute monarchy, constitutional monarchy, diarchy, elective monarchy, emirate, and a federal monarchy.

Oligarchy – A government in which the power is vested in a few persons. These people could be wealthy, powerful, and/or influential, and might share similar interests and/or family. Some other types of oligarchic governments are: ergatocracy, kritarchy, netocracy, plutocracy, stratocracy, and theocracy.

Polyarchy – A form of government in which power is vested in three or more persons. The word polyarchy is Greek for "many leaders." This could also be a triarchy, tetrarchy, or more.

Privatization – This isn't a government at all, but it can fill the functions of government. This is when the government gives a publically owned property to a privately owned business or organization. One of the most controversial ways privatization is being used today is when a government sells a land's natural water rights to a business, turning what should be a free resource to the people (fresh water) into a commodity the people have to pay for.

Republic – A government in which the power rests in the body of the citizens who are entitled to vote for representatives to exercise their will—the will of the people. Some other types of republics are: constitutional republic, democratic republic, parliamentary republic, federal republic, and a socialist republic.

Socialism – An economic system in which the production and distribution of goods are controlled by the government rather than by private enterprise. There are many varieties of socialism. Some socialists tolerate capitalism, as long as the government maintains influence over the economy. Some socialists insist on abolishing private enterprise. My understanding is that all types of communism are socialist, but not all types of socialism are communist.

Timocracy – There are two definitions for this. One is a form of government in which possession of property is required in order to hold office. The second definition is a form of government in which rulers are motivated by ambition or love of honor. Plato described it as a government in which ambition for power and glory motivates the rulers.

Totalitarian – A government that does not tolerate differing opinion and that regulates nearly every aspect of public and private life.

CYCLES OF GOVERNMENT

In *The Republic*, the Greek philosopher Plato discusses the five stages of government in descending order of moral goodness. They are: aristocracy, timocracy, oligarchy, democracy, and tyranny. Plato suggested that each regime would progressively degenerate until reaching tyranny, which when overthrown, would return to aristocracy. It's a fascinating concept. If you have some sort of rebellion or anarchy in your storyworld, you might consider Plato's argument as to what might happen next. After all, the people in a medieval-type of world who've overthrown an evil king might not come up with something like a democracy. You can read Plato's ideas yourself in *The Republic (book VIII)*, which you can download for free here: www.gutenberg.org/ebooks/1497.

KEEP IN MIND . . .

I'm not a government teacher. And you are authors. Use your imagination! Keep in mind, no government runs perfectly. In fact, not a single country today rules solely on one system of government. (Visit: www.en.wikipedia.org/wiki/File:Forms_of_government.svg for a neat Wikipedia map where you can see current types of governments in our world.)

So, combine government types and/or tweak them in regard to the storyworld, cultures, and magic you've already created. You can add negative attributes too, like having your politics influenced by entities that are not part of the formal government, like corporations, banks, mafia, thieves, mob mentality, terrorism, magical groups, wild beasts, you name it. Play around with this. Mix and match and see what you come up with. Wreak havoc!

 CREATING RELIGIONS

Every person at some point in his or her life wonders, "Where did we come from?" or "Why are we here?"

Many people believe they know the answers. Yet most of those answers are different.

Some writers don't want to deal with religion in their stories, and that's okay. But if you're seeking to create a rich and realistic world, people are going to have different beliefs about everything, especially where they came from. This is a good argument for having more than one type of religion in your book.

Religion is a system of attitudes, beliefs, and practices that address the nature of existence and purpose in the universe. Religion usually involves a moral code and ritual observances in everyday life.

As always, the amount of worldbuilding depends on your story goals. If religion plays little or no part in your plot, you don't have to do much work creating complex religions. But if religion plays a major role in your story, you'll want to put more time into it.

So what's the plot purpose of religion in your story? Maybe you'd like to write about a religious theme like death, afterlife, angels, demons, the devil, or morality. History has proved that nations with religions that have a doctrine of peace and morals become stronger than those that do not. This is likely because honest people get more business than crooked people. And people who get more business, become more powerful. Yet power has the tendency to corrupt people. This vicious cycle and the corruption of religion is a common theme throughout history.

Maybe your story is about a people group that worships trees. And maybe another people group comes in and cuts down all the trees. That would raise some serious conflict with the tree worshipping people. It might cause a war. It might cause identity crises for the religious characters. It might cause the religion to evolve into something else. Or maybe some tree worshippers will go on a quest to find more trees or to find a way to plant new ones.

Maybe you'd like to have gods as characters like The Rope and Cotillion in Steven Erikson's *Gardens of the Moon*, Torak in David Eddings's *Belgariad* series, or Mr. Wednesday in Neil Gaiman's *American Gods*.

James Cameron's *Avatar* uses religion to raise questions about one's relationship to the world around us, to one another, and, ultimately, to a higher power.

Alice Sebold's *The Lovely Bones* follows a dead girl who tries to solve her murder from a purgatory of sorts.

In *Indiana Jones and the Temple of Doom*, Indiana's search for a mystical stone leads him to an underground temple where a Kali-worshiping cult practices black magic, child slavery, and human sacrifice.

Dan Brown created alternate Christian history in *The Da Vinci Code* and turned it into a mystery/thriller novel.

The Exorcist focuses in on one aspect of Catholic Christianity as a dispirited priest is called in to perform an exorcism on a young girl.

The show *Supernatural* exploits many religious subjects and meshes them with paranormal themes as Sam and Dean Winchester continually save the day—and world.

So where do you start worldbuilding religion?

If you're writing historical fantasy or alternate history, religions played a big role in society, and it would be a mistake to leave them out from your story entirely. Research the time in which your story takes place to learn about the religions of that era and location.

But if you're creating your own religion, start by deciding what type. Monotheism? Polytheism? Monism, Dualism, or Pluralism?

Pantheon? Pantheism? Or how about nontheistic religions like Animism, Buddhism, most types of Hinduism, Jainism, or Naturalism? Religions with no gods can worship or pursue an ideal like freedom, peace, or wisdom.

Pick one of these and tweak some things. Or take two or three and combine parts of them until you come up with something interesting. Add elements from your storyworld, history, magic, and cultures to the religion as well.

Study religions of our world. Where did they come from and why do people follow them? Use what you learn to create parallels in your story. Oftentimes the level of technology comes into play with religion. Historically speaking, the more man learned about science, the less man believed in a deity. If you have very little technology in your storyworld, you'll likely have a larger population that believes in one or more higher powers. People or creatures with great power or strength might be considered gods. For example: The dragon eats us, so we worship the dragon and give it sacrifices so that we can maintain peace with the mighty dragon.

What or who do people worship and why? Does magic tie in with the religion? Is the god or gods unseen and impersonal or does he/they take an active role with the people? How are the followers organized? How do they worship? Do they have a strict diet? Do they make sacrifices? Offerings? Do they pay tithes or perform daily prayer rituals? I've always been fascinated by the Jewish phylacteries, which are little boxes that contain scrolls of parchment inscribed with verses and are tied to the arm and forehead during prayer. This practice was inspired by four verses in the Torah.

Where do the followers worship? In homes, temples, churches, or shrines? Are there priests who act as guides or intermediaries between the god and the people? If so, what does the priestly role look like? Are they strict or lenient in leading the believers? How much power do the priestly characters have? More power or less power than the political rulers?

Are there services? If so, how often? Are there required prayer times like Muslims have? Fasting? Saints? Holy books? Statues to worship? Songs? Liturgies? Are there different worshiping rules for men than for women or children? Are there secrets that a follower discovers the longer he's a member? Or is everything free to all people? Must young people go on a mission? Are there missionaries? Do the believers keep separate from nonbelievers like the Amish? Is there a symbol for the religion like the star of David or a cross? Is there an object that helps a believer pray like a rosary or an altar?

Consider having sects of the religion. No religion is in absolute agreement. Just look at Christianity and all the different denominations, branches, and even cult-versions it has. Some of the differences are over little things that don't matter to many believers, but those difference might be very important to certain people.

Also, the religions you create should have spawned heresies which would have brought about reform movements, which would have inspired some followers to rebel against reforms. This might lead to protests, the growth of orthodox or liberal movements, and possibly even war. And if certain sects were outlawed, they might go underground to worship in secret.

RELIGIOUS BIAS AND RESPECT

There are some publishers who publish books specifically for a certain religious audience. Two specialty markets I'm aware of is the Evangelical Christian Publishers Association (ECPA) and the Latter Day Saints (LDS) market. If you're writing for one of these, you can use religion more specifically, since the audience is meant to be primarily of the same religion as the author.

But if you're a religious person writing a book for the general public, try not to allow your personal beliefs to influence your story. This can be very difficult. I try to write each of my characters as honestly as I can and present each side fairly. I didn't always do the best at this in my early books, and I've offended as many people as I've thrilled. So goes the life of a writer, I suppose.

Also keep in mind that earth has many religions. Whether or not you believe with all your heart, mind, soul, and strength that Judaism or Christianity or Hinduism or Scientology or Atheism is the only truth, as an author who is trying to create a unique storyworld with diverse characters, you should strive to remain impartial. Let your characters be who they are. And if you write a character who worships a religion that you don't believe in, you owe it to that character to research his religion and portray his beliefs with fairness and respect. That's the mark of a good writer.

CREATING CONFLICT

No matter how many religions you create for your story, you should have some characters and/or people groups who believe in secularism, atheism, agnosticism, or who simply live their lives indifferent to any form of religion.

Religion can also come into conflict with government, magic, the economy, and between individuals.

If you've developed multiple religions, find a way to give them conflict with one another. For example, do you know why Jews, Muslims, and Christians fight over Jerusalem? It's because of when Abraham went up to the mountain to sacrifice his son as God asked him to do, and God sent a lamb instead. (You can read the story in Genesis 22 of the Bible. I don't know the references for the Torah or the Quran.) The problem is that Jews and Christians believe that Abraham was asked to sacrifice Isaac, the son God promised to him and his wife in their old age. And Muslims believe that Abraham was asked to sacrifice Ishmael, his firstborn son that Hagar, his wife's servant, bore to him.

Seems like no big deal, right? But hundreds of years later, God sent a prophet to King David, telling him to go and build an altar in the same place where Abraham attempted to sacrifice his son. That is where David's son Solomon built the temple in Jerusalem when he was king. Today, a mosque sits on that land. Why? Because the story of Abraham's faithfulness and God's mercy and provision is dear to three world religions, who each claim that place as their holy land. And they fight over it to this day.

That's the kind of conflict you want to create with the religions in your story.

CREATING TECHNOLOGY

As mentioned in chapter three, there are four important technologies that greatly affect a civilization: communication, medicine, vehicles, and weapons/tools. Remember, whoever has the power, controls the resources, and whoever controls the resources, controls the people. Civilizations with advanced technology usually have more power over a civilization with primitive technology.

Consider the level of advancement within each of those four areas of technology for each of the people groups in your storyworld. Remember the longbows the English used to fight the French during the Hundred Years' War? The technology levels between different people groups shouldn't be the same in your world. Play around with different combinations. Maybe your people have advanced weaponry, but their medicine is still quite primitive.

If you don't know where to start, pick one or more time and place in earth's history to use as a guide. For example, you might use the steam engines of the 1800s but say that guns have not been invented and that people still fight with swords, bows and arrows, or spears.

COMMUNICATION

If you're writing a contemporary fantasy or a futuristic science fiction story and you don't show differently, readers might assume that communication levels are the same as what we have currently.

On the other hand, if you're writing a current-day story and want communications technology to be the same as ours, don't forget to accurately make use of cell phones. Sometimes us older writers forget that no one needs a payphone or a paper map these days.

Think about the communications technology for your story. Do people use verbal communication or some primitive form of grunting and sign language? If there's verbal language, how many languages are spoken in your world? Can people speak multiple languages? If so, where do they learn?

There are other types of communications that you can use for all kinds of reasons. Maybe you need a secret way of passing messages back and forth. Or maybe you have a race without voices. In our world, people have used many methods of communicating: yodeling, body language, hand signals, the hydraulic telegraph, the heliograph, flags, semaphore lines, signal lamps, books/printing press, newspapers, the telegraph, morse code, the telephone, radio, intercoms, pneumatic tubes, video conferencing, mobile phones, email, cell phones, and texting.

When you're planning futuristic technologies, you have to think way ahead because our current technology is amazing. Ask yourself what might come next? Is faster-than-light communication possible in my world? If so, does every culture have that ability? If not, why?

Have fun brainstorming futuristic communication types. There could be robots or droids that we send out with messages. We might find a way to communicate telepathically. In my *Safe Lands* trilogy, people could purchase SimTalk implants in their ears, which were set up on a home computer, then voice-activated without the need of a cell phone or tablet.

Does your world have an Internet? Cell phones? Old school phone lines? Something more advanced like communication implants? Or something more primitive like a messenger on a horse? How fast people can communicate affects the growth of a civilization.

It also affects how well military commanders can get their jobs done. If a group of people were to travel back in time with CB radios, that communication ability might change the outcomes of many past wars.

Ancient forms of communication include fires, smoke signals, beacon huts, drums, and horns. Remember the beacons that were lit in *The Return of the King* to get the signal to Rohan?

In the Middle Ages, one could send a letter by messenger or pigeon post. Messengers could walk, ski, ride horses or camels or mules, drive dogsleds, or sail on boats.

In Georgian England, the cost of mail was calculated by how many pages and by how many miles the messenger traveled. Payment was due upon receipt by the addressee and could cost as much as a day's wages!

But in the Victorian era, flat rate post became the norm, and people so enjoyed communicating that mail carriers traveled their delivery routes as much as twelve times a day.

There are also religious forms of communication with deities like prayer, making a sacrifice, singing, or other acts of worship.

Also think about whether the people in your book write by hand, and, if so, what they write on. Cave paintings? Carving on stone tablets? Writing on leather, vellum, parchment, papyrus, or paper?

As always, once you decide what your technology is, look for ways to add conflict and plot twists. Can the communication of your world be disabled or intercepted? Do your people have to stop using it to keep from being detected by the enemy? Or perhaps a character must invent some sort of communication to aid the plot.

MEDICINE

Primitive peoples understood enough about healing to bandage wounds with bark or animal skins or pack them in mud to stop the bleeding. But they had little understanding of what illness was. Most believed illnesses came from the gods or evil spirits or from curses the enemy placed on them. That's why most had rituals to undo curses or perform healing ceremonies. Some even carried amulets to ward off sickness.

Early doctors discovered remedies for ailments in certain plants, roots, or minerals. These could be crushed into liquids or foods, or made into tonics, creams, or ointments.

Egyptians believed that there were canals inside the body and that illness blocked these canals. Because of this belief, they favored remedies like inhaling steam, inducing vomiting, and taking laxatives.

In ancient Greece, many believed in the gods of healing and spent plenty of money to visit temples and purchase "cures." Greeks believed that the body was made up of elements, and if they were in balance, the person should be healthy.

Aristotle introduced the idea that the body was made up of four humors: blood, phlegm, black bile, and yellow bile. If a person was ill, it was believed he had too much of one area and needed to be rid of it. Some believed in treating illnesses with opposites. If the patient had a fever, they needed to intake cold substances. If a patient had chills, he needed to intake hot liquids or spicy foods.

The Romans learned that dirty water and sewage brought on illnesses. They developed aqueducts to bring clean water to the city, drained swamps or ponds of water they believed was unhealthy, and built sewer systems to carry waste out of the city via underground streams.

When Rome fell, much medical knowledge was lost. Ill medieval Europeans suffered centuries of bloodletting, purging, and having the color, smell, and taste of their urine examined. Some believed disease was caused by seeds blown on the wind or passed on by touch. Barbers pulled teeth, set broken bones, and performed amputations and simple surgeries. Artificial limbs might have been made from wood or bone. Some ascribed importance to Zodiac signs and superstitions surrounding them. Some believed illnesses could be cured by a king's touch. Folk remedies were likely one of the safest forms of medicine at that time.

Eventually, medieval doctors rejected magic and superstition and focused on observing a patient and giving herbal remedies.

Sometimes the sick were mistreated or abused. The very sick were often quarantined. Lepers were forced to live in colonies. Some believed that the mentally ill were not truly human or were evil. Many were locked up in institutions, some kept in irons.

The invention of the microscope changed the face of medicine, followed by the discovery of vaccinations; the invention of the stethoscope; and the discovery and understanding of germs, immunizations, anesthetics, insulin, antibiotics, and drugs. All this eventually led to the use of artificial organs; the ability to conduct difficult surgeries, transplants, and artificial inseminations; and the use of fiber optics, CAT scans, and MRIs to enable doctors to see inside the patient's body.

Think over this history and let it inspire ways you might use medicine in your story. In my book *Captives*, the people of the Safe Lands are dying from a plague. All searches for a cure have failed. This forces them to kidnap uninfected individuals to study, something they never considered doing before. But they're desperate. They want to survive.

You could have a people with advanced technology, but if they have terrible health care, they're at risk. So consider medicine as an aspect you can play with in storyworld creation that has the potential for great conflict.

VEHICLES

What has been invented in your world? Does the wheel exist? The raft? Have animals been domesticated? If things are more advanced, how much so? Does your world have the steam engine? The electric engine? Some form of air travel? Space travel?

How are your roads? The first roads were trails created by humans walking from place to place. Poor roads kept kingdoms from expanding. Rome built excellent roads so that their army could travel. But later on, in the Middle Ages, the roads were simple dirt paths that became flooded or so muddy in spring that carts would get stuck. Does your world have canals and bridges that make it cheaper and faster to transport goods?

And how are goods and people transported? Domestic animals were trained to carry cargo on their backs, in packs, or in saddlebags.

A travois consisted of two poles lashed together to create a sled-like frame to drag things. Litters were chairs or little houses lashed to poles that could be carried by men or animals.

Are the roadways managed? Are there tolls to cross bridges or travel roads? Are there groups of men who guard and maintain these to keep them in good shape and to protect those who travel them?

What about other technologies that aid travel? Like the compass or rudders on ships? Has someone invented the steam engine in your storyworld? Or are people still riding horses? Keep in mind, horses can only travel about thirty miles a day, walking. If they're run ragged, they can go between fifty and sixty miles a day—but then they're spent. Beware of having horses run like Galdalf's did in *The Return of the King*. Shadowfax was a special breed of horse; most horses could never ride like he did.

In science fiction, you must decide whether faster-than-light transportation exists, and, if so, does every culture have that ability? Are there any other ways to travel in the future? Think about the transporters in *Star Trek*, portals in *Stargate*, or the Doctor's time-traveling T.A.R.D.I.S.

You can also play with some of the technologies that scientists are currently exploring, like turning tethered satellites into space elevators, creating supercavitating watercraft, finding inexpensive ways to power vacuum tubes. If you don't know what these things are, Google them. Here are some more: magnetic levitation (mag-lev) systems, solar-powered bullet trains, "wing in ground" low-flying aircrafts, gravitational time dilation, road trains, human-powered monorails, and flying cars.

WEAPONS & TOOLS

What has been invented to make life easier or safer? Are people making containers out of pottery and clay? Have they discovered how to make glass? Or are they capable of making things out of metals?

Have they discovered the concepts of simple machines like the inclined plane, lever, pulley, screw, the wedge, and the wheel and axle? Such machines make work much easier.

Have they invented the necessary tools to put animals to work, like collars, bits, and saddles?

How about more complex machines like mills (wind or water), plows, pumps, cranks, forges, spinning wheels, clocks, or the printing press?

Have eyeglasses been invented? How about the spyglass or telescope?

What about weapons? The club, spear, axe, bow and arrow, sword, pike, mace, dagger, sling, throwing spear, longbow, catapult, Greek fire, crossbow, siege engine, trebuchet . . . Do they have shields or armor? What's it made from? Early armor was made of quilted cotton, then leather, wood, or a combination. Then chain armor. Later plates of steel. And most recently, bullet-proof vests.

Has someone invented the gun? Or are your people still using swords? If guns are available, what kind? Matchlock? Wheel lock? Flintlock? Caplock? Breech loading? Guns with cartridges? Guns with bayonets? Guns with magazines? Revolvers? Exploding shells? Machine guns? Grenades? Rockets? Bombs?

Or maybe you've created a new type of weapon that's distinctive to one of the people groups in your story.

Also think about warfare techniques: charioteers, the Saxon shield wall, the Trojan horse, the testudo formation of the Romans, a cavalry charge, pikes and longbowmen to resist cavalry, battleships with rams on the prow, fire arrows, siege engine missiles, battering rams, siege towers, unassailable forts and castles with moats and drawbridges, ladders to climb walls, tunnels dug under walls, trench raiding, a blitzkrieg, flamethrowers, mines, tanks, sub-machine guns, and submarines.

When both sides have somewhat equal weapons or one side is inferior, people come up with different techniques to achieve victory. In the past, poisoning water sources with dead bodies was a common tactic. In the first world war, poisonous gas were one of the most feared of all weapons for the way it killed, putting its victims in agony for days to weeks before they died. This resulted in soldiers wearing gas masks.

Over time bombs and missiles grew deadlier until the fear of them forced a certain level of peace. Is there peace in your world?

If your story is futuristic, what kinds of things have been invented that add to your character's way of life? Can he hydrate a pizza like in *Back To the Future*? Does he have a phone built into his hand like in the new *Total Recall*? Spray-on healing like in Stephanie Meyer's *Host*? Has Taco Bell taken over every restaurant like in *Demolition Man*? Do cars drive themselves like in *Minority Report*? Are there food replicators like in *Star Trek*? In my *Safe Lands* series, one can get SimArt tags imbedded under the skin to reflect virtual tattoos.

What about weapons technology? Might your world have some kind of instant healing armor? Robot police officers like in *Robocop*? Stormtroopers? Robots? AI? Heat rays like in *The War of the Worlds*? Induced hallucinations to train soldiers like in *Divergent*? Or how about the way the Capitol in *The Hunger Games* used different types of mutations (jabberjays, tracker jackers, wolf mutts, etc.) as offensive tools? The only limit here is your imagination.

PLAY WITH IT

How might the technology come into conflict with different cultures in your world? In *Dune*, off-world people are fighting for control of the planet Arrakis. We later find out that the natives—the people that the Emperor thought were primitive—really weren't. They knew how to live in the desert, and they had developed amazing technology to grow plants and had learned to ride the worms. They kept that a secret because it served their best interests for the Emperor to think they were not a threat.

In my *Blood of Kings* storyworld, those gifted in bloodvoicing can communicate with their minds, no matter the distance. They can also slip into the Veil and instantly see any place they've been before. They're invisible there, but their physical bodies aren't able to travel with them. Still, this level of communication and being able to spy on an enemy greatly helps in a battle.

Technology is important in way-of-life activities too. I was writing a dinner scene in *To Darkness Fled* and realized I didn't know if silverware had yet been invented in my world. I later decided that different peoples could be at different levels of advancement in regards to eating utensils. So when Achan ate dinner in Mirrorstone with Lord Eli, he had never seen anything like the plates his host served food on, so to him, they were ceramic trenchers.

When you go back through to edit your novel, watch to make sure that your technology matches what you've set up in your storyworld, and look for interesting ways to add conflict.

10 CREATING LANGUAGES

I'm not much of an advocate for creating your own language—at least not the way Tolkien did it. If you think it would be fun and you want to, go for it. But every time you use a made-up language in your novel, you risk annoying your readers and pulling them out of the story. Plus, many editors are wary of fantasy novels that are thick with fictional languages.

So this chapter comes with a strong caution. You should create your culture first. Work hard on who the people are, then think of a language to complement them. Make sure that the language doesn't take over your story. Also avoid putting translations in parenthesis.

This is risky business, indeed.

Yet I must confess: I created a language for my *Blood of Kings* trilogy. I didn't create much, maybe a total of twenty words. It was the Eben language, and it was first spoken in book one, *By Darkness Hid*, when Vrell, Jax, and Khai entered the Nahar Forest and came across some Eben giants. Here's an excerpt:

> Vrell peeked around the tree to see a man as tall as Jax, but pale as a lily. His long blond hair hung around his face like a curtain. Animal skins were draped over one shoulder, across his white chest, and down around his hips like a skirt. He clutched a spear in one hand and a curved axe in

the other. Both weapons were chiseled out of obsidian and lashed to wooden handles with leather. He stood on the road facing Jax.

Jax bowed to the giant. "We seek passage through Nahar Forest."

The giant pointed down the road, back toward Walden's Watch. "*Wee ahlawa men teeah!*"

Jax shook his head. "We will not go back. We must take this road to Xulon."

The pale giant tipped his head back and bellowed a trilling cry into the treetops.

Since Vrell doesn't speak Eben—or even know what an Eben is at this point in the story, she can't translate. Jax can, but he doesn't. The reader can pick up on the translation based on Jax's response to the giant. Here's another section of Eben dialogue I used in book two, *To Darkness Fled*:

"Who sent you?" Sir Gavin yelled.

The raspy breathing of a dying Eben was the only answer. Achan inched over the lichen until the men came into view. Sir Gavin crouched on the giant's right, blade held to the pale throat. Sir Caleb and Inko stood panting on the giant's left side.

Sir Gavin pressed a knee on the giant's chest. "Who?"

The giant's ragged breath seemed to consume all his effort, but he blinked slowly and turned his dark eyes to Achan, his voice a raspy growl. "*Tee saplaway sen katla sar.*"

The intensity in that gaze shook Achan's knees. The man had a black insignia inked onto his forehead, three lines, each thicker than the first.

"I know why you've come," Sir Gavin said, "I want to know who sent you."

"*Faluk san.*"

In this scene, I used Sir Gavin in the same way that I used Jax.

Sir Gavin speaks Eben. Achan does not. But there's no need for me to put in a translation. That would mess up the intensity of the scene, which I'm already risking with the use of my made-up language.

I do, however, have a translation in my story bible notes. Here's how the Eben language works.

VERBS PHRASES I MADE UP

to take: *finla*
to go: *ahla*
to come: *sapla*
to do: *katla*
to be: *badla*

OTHER WORDS

there: *men*
here: *sen*
prince: *sar*
you: *wee*
I/we: *tee*
away: *teeah*

GRAMMATICAL PARTICLE

In Eben, particles modify nouns to indicate tense. I got the idea for this from the Japanese language, though my language works differently. For example, "*wa*" indicates the present tense of a verb, and "*way*" indicates past tense. Therefore, the first example above, "*Wee ahlawa men teeah!*" is translated: "Go back where you came from." But literally, here's how it works:

Wee	*ahla-*	*wa*	*men*	*teeah!*
You	to go	present tense	back	away

And the second example sentence:

Tee	*sapla-*	*way*	*sen*	*katla*	*sar.*
I/we	to come	present tense	here	to take	prince

The whole thing is such nerdly fun, isn't it?

THINGS TO CONSIDER WHEN
CREATING YOUR OWN LANGUAGE

1. What do you need? If you only need a few sentences like I did with Eben (all my language notes fit on one sheet of paper), you don't need to create a full translation of your language to English.

2. Choose some base words, like nouns and pronouns. I started with writing the dialogue I needed translated and then thought up words for that. You'll definitely want words for: he, she, I, you, we. You might also want to create numbers one through ten.

3. Make up some verbs and decide how you'll conjugate them in your language. Consider creating prefixes or suffixes to alter tense. Languages are based on rules, and so should yours be. Look at other languages for examples and inspiration.

4. Create suffixes or prefixes for other things like: plurals and endings like –ly, –ful, –er, –ed, –ent, –able, –ing, –ness, etc.

5. Look for ways to add consistency and sound patterns that will set your language apart from other languages. Think of how distinctive the French language sounds from Asian languages. For my Eben language, all of my verbs ended in "*la.*" And I made certain words similar: "here" (*sen*) and "there" (*men*); "I"/"we" (*tee*) and "you" (*wee*). English has the "–ing" that makes verbs active and sound similar and the "–ed" for past tense.

6. Write some sentences in different forms and tenses, then come up with how they'll be said differently. Use that same format for all verbs. For example: I walked to the house. She walked to the house. We ran to the house. They walked away from the house.

7. Simple is best. Most English words aren't difficult to pronounce, at least not for pronouns and verbs. Go easy on the

accents, apostrophes, and dashes. (Avoid them altogether?) Don't make your words so hard to pronounce that your reader can't even read them.

That would be bad.

Remember, cool is great for creatures and magic and storyworld elements. But with languages, simple is best.

YOU CAN ALSO. . .

•Create an alphabet.
•Create a pronunciation guide for certain letter combinations.
•Create symbols for your alphabet.
•Use a dictionary to help you know what words you might need to create translations for.
•Name your language.
•Practice speaking it to other people.

But most of that is going *way* overboard. If you really want to invent a new language more than you want to write your story, have fun. Just make sure that when you come back to put the language into your story, it enhances things and doesn't take over.

11 VERNACULAR LANGUAGE

Plain, everyday, ordinary speech is called vernacular language. This includes analogies, euphemisms, idioms, metaphors, and similes; curses and insults; quotes and songs; and dialect.

RHETORICAL LANGUAGE

You're likely familiar with clichés. They could be idioms, which are impossible phrases like, "It's raining cats and dogs," expressions like, "there's a method to my madness," metaphors like "alabaster skin," or other phrases that have been overused. In fact, these sayings have been used so much they either make the reader roll his eyes or they're invisible and add nothing to your story.

Here are a few you might recognize:

We're all in the same boat.
The soldiers were dropping like flies.
The third time's a charm.
She'd give her right arm to get that.
She had cherry red lips.
He smelled like rotten eggs.

There are so many of those types of sayings, I could go on for pages. I'm guilty of having used clichés in my books. Some of these phrases are so common that I don't even realize I use them until I catch them in rewrites or after a book is published. Ack!

How can you avoid these? Search your writing for cliché phrases and make them your own. Tweak them a little—or a lot—using your storyworld details. This can be an excellent way to reveal your worldbuilding and plant good questions in the reader's mind.

In doing this, you might completely change the syntax of the cliché, but it can also be fun to keep the syntax so that readers might catch on to what you've done. For example:

We're all in the same boat. --> We're all in the same escape pod. (For a science fiction story.)

The soldiers were dropping like flies. --> The soldiers were dropping like spark stones. (For a world that rains spark stones. Or this could have something to do with the world's magic.)

The third time's a charm. --> The fifth time's all the luck. (For a world that is superstitious about the number five.)

She'd give her right arm to get that. --> He'd give his two left legs to get that. (For a world in which people have multiple legs.)

She had cherry red lips. --> She had lips like a fire berry. (Gives the opportunity to mention fire berries and describe something. The reader will likely assume that fire berries are red.)

He smelled like rotten eggs. --> He smelled like the river end of a privy chute. (Speaks for itself. Eww.)

The voice of your character matters a great deal too. As well as the situation.

She was drunk as a skunk. --> The glutton sponge poisoned herself with drink. (A woman's voice, perhaps gossiping with others.)

She was drunk as a skunk. --> She kept falling like a baby lamb. (A child's voice.)

She was drunk as a skunk. --> She was mind-mangled enough not to remember her name—or mine. (A man's voice, perhaps bragging to friends.)

CURSES AND INSULTS

I'm not a fan of swearing in mythical storyworlds, even coming from a profane character. It disrupts my immersion in the storyworld when the F-word starts showing up. In a book that takes place in our world, this type of swearing makes sense. But characters from another world wouldn't use earthly swear words.

Another problem with swearing in fiction is that so many writers use it gratuitously, not bothering to take into account characters who wouldn't use coarse language. This can pull readers out of the story. It can also alienate a host of readers who don't like it and even some publishers (always do your homework before submitting).

A good writer can show a profane character without ever using a real-life curse word. But if you want to put swearing in your novel, remember that less is more. Save those words for the time when they will have the biggest impact. If you use them on every page, it becomes a gimmick.

I prefer to have my characters curse with words that mean something to their storyworld. Here are some I used in my *Blood of Kings* trilogy.

My main character often yelled or muttered, "Pig snout!" It was his catch phrase. No other character used it.

One of my knights who was from a land with an active volcano used the curse, "Fire and ash!" when he was angry.

Some common phrases were: "For Lightness' sake!" (My land is half cursed in Darkness.) Or "For Cetheria's hand!" (Cetheria is the goddess of protection.) Some of the knights used the phrase "Eben's breath!" as a general curse. (An Eben is an ugly giant.) Many bloodvoicers used the phrases "I'll be stormed" or "I'll be ransomed." (In my storyworld "storming" is when you force someone from their body in a telepathic battle, and "ransomed" is to be rescued by the One God.)

Some other phrases I used: "Blazes!" "What in flames?" and "I don't give a pig's eye about . . . (fill in the blank)."

Here are some curses, slang words, or phrases you might recognize from books, television, or movies. Can you guess the references? Look for the answers in the Extras section.

Zark
Sweet mother of Artemis!
Son of a hamster!
Smoke you.
Oh, my prophetic soul!
Sleemo
Mudblood
Bit brain
Cowpog
Shattering Glass!
Shiitake mushrooms!
Frak!

QUOTES AND SONGS

In fantasy fiction, songs you write for your story are usually referred to as doggerel. The word doggerel came from the late fourteenth century as a word that meant "bad poetry fit only for dogs." Kind of harsh, really. Today it also can refer to any kind of poetry or songs used in fiction.

Don't be offended that the definition of doggerel calls our stunning words "bad poetry." It just so happens that, for the most part, we aren't writing poems to stagger the literary world or songs that will win Grammys. We're writing poems or songs to add to our storyworld.

Here is an excerpt from one you may recognize:

> "Dump the crocks in a boiling bowl;
> Pound them up with a thumping pole;
> And when you've finished if any are whole,
> Send them down the hall to roll!

That's what Bilbo Baggins hates!
So, carefully! carefully with the plates!"

That example was from *The Hobbit*, of course. Tolkien used a lot of doggerel in his books. I had fun writing such things for my *Blood of Kings* trilogy. Here are three excerpts from three different songs.

"Hail the piper, fiddle, fife,
The night is young and full of life.
The Corner teems with ale and song.
And we shall dance the whole night long."

"View not my face, I am undone beside you.
The beating of my heart will not cease.
Whilst I am near you, whilst I am near you."

"He grew up here in Sitna Town,
The hand his life was dealt.
He milked the goats and fetched the wood,
Or Poril gave him the belt."

Be careful not to overdo it with songs. Too many of them, and readers will start skimming. In fact, I've met readers who tell me they never read songs in books.

Never.

Once you've written songs or poems, you can have other characters quote them. Or you can simply make up quotes for your books. Frank Herbert does this in his novel *Dune* with quotes from ancient writings at the head of each new chapter.

DIALECT

Dialect is the way a person speaks that is distinguished by his culture, social group, or the region in which he lives. His speech pattern is different from other varieties of the same language by vocabulary, pronunciation, and grammar.

Authors change the way certain characters talk to set them apart from other characters. This is very important in historical genres, whether they be straight historical fiction or speculative varieties like historical fantasy or alternate history. Here are some examples of historical or regional dialect done well:

"... Don't let me hear no more of you, or you shall feel some more of me. D'ye hear?"

"I warn't doing no harm," Young Jerry protested, rubbing his cheek.

"Drop it then," said Mr. Cruncher; "I won't have none of *your* no harms. Get a top of that there seat, and look at the crowd."

—From *A Tale of Two Cities* by Charles Dickens, a novel drawn from historical events of the revolutionary period in France. Jerry Cruncher speaks with a common dialect, full of slang and satire.

"This is not to be borne! Miss Bennet, I insist on being satisfied. Has he, my nephew, made you an offer of marriage?"

"Your ladyship has declared it to be impossible."

"It ought to be so; it must be so, while he retains the use of his reason. But your arts and allurements may, in a moment of infatuation, have made him forget what he owes to himself and to all his family. You may have drawn him in."

"If I have, I shall be the last person to confess it."

—From *Pride and Prejudice* by Jane Austen. Most of Austen's main characters are English gentry during Regency England.

"I'm—er—not supposed ter do magic, strictly speakin'. I was allowed ter do a bit ter follow yeh an' get yer letters to yeh an' stuff—one o' the reasons I was so keen ter take on the job."

"Why aren't you supposed to do magic?" asked Harry.

"Oh, well—I was at Hogwarts meself but I—er—got expelled, ter tell yeh the truth. In me third year. They snapped me wand in half an' everything."

—From *Harry Potter and the Sorcerer's Stone* by J. K. Rowling. Hagrid's accent is a contemporary West-country English accent.

"Now, you vill come to verk for me here for eight months und zen you vill buy vone off my camelts, und I vill teach you to train zem and you vill get two vild vones und dat vill be dat. I haf just de animal for you. He hass only vone eye but, ha, dat does not matter—he is stronk and reliable enough for you, ya."

—From *Tracks* by Robyn Davidson. The speaker, Kurt Posel, is a contemporary German Australian.

If you need to write a certain dialect, study it by reading works from that time period or by listening to people speak on YouTube or in movies and transcribing their words.

If you're merely seeking to tweak a person's language, you might play with spelling, word choice, or syntax to create different dialects. Here are some that I've done or seen done in fiction:

•Stuttering by breaking up words with hyphens, and dragging out or repeating letters like Ts, Ps, Ss, or whichever letter(s) you choose to have your character stumble over. For example: P-pleassse p-passs the s-ssalt.

•Avoiding contractions to give a more formal tone to dialogue.

•Replacing the G from –ing endings with an apostrophe.

•Lisps shown by replacing all the Ss with a TH.

•The use of bad grammar like ain't, gonna, and wanna.

•Word choice. I'm from Alaska, and we Alaskans refer to snow mobiles as "snow machines." I've been mocked repeatedly for this. I also refer to hair bands as "rubber bands" or "hair ties," while teens call them "ponytails." Word choice also differs between generations.

•Pronunciation. I always say the word elementary as "elemen-tair-ee," whereas my husband says, "elemen-tree."

•Foreign words. I have a Latina friend who, whenever she says a Spanish word, says that word in a thick accent. She also uses some foreign words over the English ones, like when she refers to her brother as *mi hermano*.

•The syntax or word order when writing foreigners speaking English. Yoda also speaks with a rearranged word order.

When I worked on the Russian characters for my novel *The New Recruit*, I listened to many Russians speaking English, and I took notes, sometimes even transcribing their words so that I could see the word order they used. Here is an example of a Russian speaking English from *The New Recruit*:

> "These three apartment are for you stay." He motioned to the door behind him, then the ones on either side. "Boys will be taking first room, girls will be taking last. Between is kitchen, TV, and room for Stopplecamp family. When you are settled, come to kitchen. My wife is preparing dinner."

The risk in writing dialects into your character's voice is that some are so difficult to read that one must read them again and again to gain understanding. And that pulls readers out of the story.

We don't want to do that to our readers. Fiction is about immersing them in our world. When we do that well, we get emails from readers who accuse us of keeping them up all night.

We want that. We want lots of it.

So take care and don't overdo this. A little goes a long way. Don't give a unique dialect to every character. Make sure the dialect, word choices, and slang matches the character's voice. Also make sure you're consistent with each character's dialogue, because inconsistencies can also pull readers from your story.

12 WORLDS WITHIN OUR WORLD

What if you're writing a speculative fiction novel that takes place on earth? Do you still need to spend time worldbuilding?

Yep.

Think about Camp Half-Blood in the *Percy Jackson* books and all the planning that must have gone into combining Greek mythology with today's culture.

The early part of Neil Gaiman's *Stardust* takes place in the 1850's English village of Wall. Tristran crosses the wall and enters the magical land of Faerie, where stars are living creatures who are hunted for their hearts.

In the *Harry Potter* series, the entire wizarding world took an incredible amount of worldbuilding. From Hogwarts and the other wizarding schools to the intricacies of Ministry of Magic, right down to using paper airplanes for memos rather than owls, since the birds were making a mess.

If the novel is historical, you must do your research to accurately show the time period. That research becomes a big part of your storyworld. If the novel is contemporary, you need to research the locations.

But after that, the same rules apply in building a storyworld. You still need to come up with all of the things that makes your novel speculative. Start with the storyworld elements that are tied closely to your plot and work from there.

PROGRESSION OF BELIEF

When an everyday, regular person gets sucked into a fantasy world, there must be a moment when he realizes, "This is no joke. This is really happening to me!" That is called the progression of belief.

This is important in contemporary fantasy stories. It's a process the main character must go through, and it helps the reader as well. As the main character comes to believe, so does the reader. This progression should be gradual.

In the *Harry Potter* books, strange things have often happened in Harry's life, and the year he turns eleven years old, owls begin to deliver letters addressed to him. But it's not until Harry sees Hagrid do magic that he starts to believe. And it's not until he passes into Diagon Alley that he sees *and* believes.

In *The Lightning Thief*, Percy's substitute teacher turns into a fury (a monster), and Percy believes that something strange is going on. Mr. Brunner gives him a pen, which he calls a "powerful weapon," and tells Grover to take Percy and his mom to Camp Half-Blood. On the way, they're attacked by a minotaur. Grover tells Percy to, "Use the pen!" Then later, when Percy wakes up in Camp Half-Blood, sees that Grover is a satyr, Mr. Brunner is a centaur, and is told his father is Poseidon, he sees *and* believes.

If you're writing this kind of story, make sure you give your hero this progression that leads to seeing and believing the world is real.

GIVE HIM THE TOUR

Another important component in an earthly fantasy is, that once the main character believes, he usually gets a tour. Or at least a short explanation. Harry Potter gets several tours. First he sees Diagon Alley, and Hagrid gives him some details. Harry makes friends with Ron and Hermione, who are there to fill him in on the things he doesn't know about the wizarding world. At school all the first year students get sorted, then the head boy of each house takes them to their dorms. All this serves as a good way to show the reader everything he needs to learn about the storyworld.

As the author, you need to know how the world works to be able to write these scenes. The first chapter of *Harry Potter and the Sorcerer's Stone* is from Mr. Dursley's point of view, and he mentions all the owls and the people dressed in strange robes and hats. Later we learn that most wizards don't go around in public all that often. They tend to keep to themselves, away from muggles. They place enchantments and illusions over business and homes and schools so that muggles might not accidentally stumble upon them. The Ministry of Magic is underground and one can get there through the phone booth or by floo powder. Platform 9 3/4 is magical, and to get into it, you have to run at the pillar between platforms 9 and 10 at the King's Cross station in London. These details don't come to us all at once or in an all-encompassing prologue. They are interspersed into the story, carefully placed right where they need to be.

So think about your world. Can regular people see it? Is it right under their noses? Or is it set apart where most people won't just happen by, like Camp Half-Blood or Hogwarts? Are there secret entrances? If so, how do they work? Maybe your world is in the clouds like *Sky High*. Or maybe it's underground like the Lower Elements where the fairies live in the *Artemis Fowl* books.

A FUTURE EARTH

Maybe your story takes place in a future earth. Maybe it's here on the planet or out in space. In my *Safe Lands* series, I set the story in the year 2080 in the remains of Crested Butte, Colorado. I built a future city there too. But I researched the current weather, climates, vegetation, wildlife, rainfall, and snowfall for Crested Butte, Colorado. I drew my map of the Safe Lands over the top of the Crested Butte ski resort map. I kept some of the same street names that are there today. I also used the names of ski trails as names of hotels, restaurants, or houses. It was pretty fun.

Brandon Sanderson did something similar in *Steelheart*, which takes place in a futuristic Chicago called Newcago. There, super villains have taken over the world and coated the city in steel. It's pretty sweet, and a great example about how to build a futuristic storyworld on earth.

13 STORYWORLD BUILDER'S DISEASE

When I wrote my first fantasy novel, I got really into the whole worldbuilding thing. I drew the map, named the cities, created family trees for the ruling lord in each city, wrote out a history for my land and a description of each city, re-drew my map, researched the animals and plant life that went with each type of climate and matched them with my cities, used Photoshop to design a banner for each of my noble families, drew floor plans of castles, got lost for a while researching types of swords, bought wood to make my own waster swords, tried talking my husband into practicing swordplay with me and my waster swords, then—since I'd been a fashion design major—I thought it might be fun to draw the clothing for some of my main characters.

It was during one such fashion coloring moment that my husband said, "I thought you were going to write a book."

I looked around at the mounds of papers, the piles of markers, the ink stains on my hands from so much drawing. I looked at the stack of encyclopedias on the floor at the foot of my bed and the binder in which I had started to organize all of these things.

I realized that I might have gone too far.

I looked up at my husband, Prismacolor marker paused above my pad of art paper. I thought about his words for a moment, what they really meant, and I said, "Oh. Yeah."

An early drawing of Lord Nathak

So, after nearly three months of playing with my storyworld, my husband knocked some sense into me. I set aside my piles of planning and started to write. Good thing my husband had said something. If he hadn't, I might still be playing around with that storyworld today!

What happened to me is a common tale. This is what's affectionately known to science fiction and fantasy writers as Storyworld Builder's Disease. It happens to the best of us. Because it's fun to make up a new world. It can suck you in. And you can get lost there for a very long time.

Some people like it there. You never have to actually do any writing in that place. It's all the fun with none of the work. Well, maybe *some* work.

Don't get me wrong. Taking the time to brainstorm your storyworld is important and good. It makes it easier for you to write your book, and it makes your storyworld feel more authentic to your reader.

But it's not good to stay there forever. So if you're stuck in such a place right now, ask yourself, "Do I want to write a book or what?" Because if you do, then you've got to stop playing and do the hard work of writing that book.

So take the time you need to build your storyworld to a certain point, but give yourself a deadline and make a list of necessary worldbuilding areas you need to know for your plot. When you finish those things, stop. And write! You can always go back and do more worldbuilding. But if you get lost forever with a terminal case of Storyworld Builder's Disease, we'll never get to read your staggering work of genius.

And that would be sad.

14 HOW TO KEEP TRACK OF IT ALL

Building a storyworld is a lot of work, and you need to keep your information organized. But what works for one person might not work for another. Some people like to create a story bible, which simply means keeping everything in one place so that, when you need it, you can find it.

When I was in the depths of Storyworld Builder's Disease from worldbuilding my *Blood of Kings* books, I started putting my piles of papers into a huge three-ring binder. I added tabbed dividers for each city, for characters charts and drawings, and for my different research topics. I put the most important papers in the front. And when I needed something, the binder was right there beside me.

Since the process worked so well, I used the same method for my *Mission League* books and my *Safe Lands* books. But I've found that sometimes I just can't find that one sheet of paper I so desperately need. It's lost. Or maybe I forgot to put it in the binder. Or I might have taken it out for some reason. Not being able to find it makes me crazy, and I always loose precious writing time on the search.

So I'm trying something new with my *Kinsman* series. I've created my story bible in Microsoft Word, mostly because I'm obsessed with Word's "Find" function. I figure I can find something a lot faster with the help of a computer than leafing through a massive binder or piles of papers that have yet to make it into that binder.

Here is a screenshot of my *Kinsman* story bible. I created a different section for history, setting, magic, religions, plot, and characters, formatting them each as a Heading 1. Then I use the other heading sizes to make sub-headings and can easily click from one to the other by using the navigation menu on the left.

The red circle in the middle of the image below shows you where to change the heading type. The red circle on the right shows you where to click on "Find." This will bring up the navigation menu, which appears on the left-hand side of the image below. If you don't see the navigation menu, the red circle on the left shows you where to click to see the list of headings in your document.

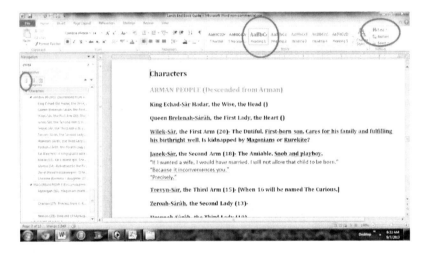

I can put all the same information into this Word story bible as I put into my 3-ring binders. I can even paste in images, write out descriptions of characters, keep track of my rules for magic, or write out the styles of worship for each of my religions. Adding multiple book headings allows me to make notes when ideas for sequels pop into my head. And I can switch between it all at the click of a button.

Very handy.

Story bibles aren't the only way to keep track of your worldbuilding data. Another thing I like to do is make a Pinterest board for my project. I can pin anything I want to that board and not only can I easily find the website again, it's a fun way that my readers can see what I'm working on.

Many of my friends rave about Scrivener. I've recently started using it, and it saves a lot of time. You can write your book in Scrivener, and keep all your notes and images in the same file as your book. And when you're done, you can export to a Word file or create ebooks in .mobi or .epub formats. Learn more about Scrivener here: www.literatureandlatte.com/scrivener.php.

Some people love to use Randy Ingermanson's Snowflake Pro software to keep track of their book information. You can learn more about that at: www.advancedfictionwriting.com/product/snowflake-pro-software.

Others enjoy Wikidpad, which allows you to create a Wikipedia-like file for your book and link between articles. This is similar to what I do with Word. You can learn more about Wikidpad here: www.sourceforge.net/projects/wikidpad.

No matter what you decide, being organized can save you lots of time when you finally sit down to write that book.

15 INTEGRATING STORYWORLD

At this point, you've spent a lot of time building your storyworld. You may even have recently been cured of Storyworld Builder's Disease. Now you're finally writing the book, but the pieces aren't falling into place! How do you use all the cool stuff you've created? Where does it fit into your story without turning your book into an epic info dump? Do you need an index of terms? A prologue that explains the backstory? How do you deal with all this? What first?

DON'T PANIC

It's great that you know so much about your storyworld. But don't try to get it perfect when you're writing your first draft. The first-draft stage is the time to get the skeleton of the story down. So, write the thing, even if it's a mess.

I like to write the book as if my reader is from my storyworld and already knows what it's like to live there. If I assume he knows the world, it keeps me from oversharing. Yes, I'll have to fix some things during the rewrite stage, but less is more, so I like to start with less. Plus, readers are smart. They'll pick up on quite a bit from the dialogue and actions of the characters.

STORY IS KEY

Your first goal is to entertain your reader. You may have created the coolest storyworld ever, but if you don't have amazing characters and a gripping plot, no one will likely care. Hopefully you've purposely built your storyworld elements around your plot and characters. Focus on writing a strong story apart from the storyworld. If you have that, and you add a great storyworld to it, you will hook those readers.

WAYS TO SHOW STORYWORLD

Your characters will experience the world as they work their way through the action of the story. So without even trying, you will have shown a great deal of your storyworld just by writing. Here are some other ways to integrate your worldbuilding.

•Look for places where your character can observe interesting scenery, plant life, beasts, weapons, vehicles, or magic. Think about when Lucy Pevensie first enters Narnia. She experiences the wonder of passing through the wardrobe and into a snowy forest. Her feet crunch over the snow, then she stops to wonder over the lamppost.

•Show your character interacting with the world. Continuing with the example from *The Lion, the Witch, and the Wardrobe* by C. S. Lewis, Mr. Tumnus arrives, he and Lucy have a short conversation, and he invites Lucy to tea. While they talk, the reader learns important things about this place: animals wear clothing, they can talk, they have manners, Mr. Tumnus refers to Lucy as a Daughter of Eve, he mentions the great castle of Cair Paravel, and he says it has been winter in Narnia for a long time. And that's before tea even starts!

This doesn't have to be a newcomer to a world, either. You can show characters observing and interacting with a world they know well. Think of *Cinder* by Marissa Meyer. The story starts with Cinder removing her foot. Through that action, the reader sees what life is like for this cyborg girl.

•Let your characters talk about the world. George R. R. Martin does this so simply in his *Song of Ice and Fire* series with his phrase, "Winter is coming." Another great example of this is in Maggie Stiefvater's *The Scorpio Races*. The characters talk about the upcoming races, how dangerous they are, which are the best and most lethal of the *capaill uisce*, who'll win, etc. All that helps the reader understand the world.

•Merge world and character motivation. Going back to Lucy Pevensie in Narnia, she's eager to bring her siblings to meet Mr. Tumnus. Her first attempt fails, which frustrates her when her siblings think she made it up. So she goes back on her own, and Edmund follows. Lucy's motivation here is to prove she isn't crazy, Edmund's is curiosity. Both bring us back into Narnia.

•Merge world with plot and conflict. In Narnia, Edmund meets the Queen, who bribes him with a box full of Turkish Delight to bring his siblings to her. Later Lucy refers to the Queen as the White Witch, and now we have conflict within Edmund. What will he do?

•Let your characters use rhetorical language, slang, curses, insults, and songs that show storyworld details.

•Consider having a character interested in science, who enjoys studying the world around him.

•Bring in a character from another part of the world who can observe differences from home and maybe even ask questions. Ani from the *Goose Girl* becomes one of those characters when she first comes to live in Bayern.

The trick to doing this well is learning to give subtle clues to your worldbuilding, and whenever possible, to make these clues part of the action.

MAGIC HAPPENS IN THE REWRITE

Once you've written your first draft and have taken a good look at your characters and plot, it's time to look for more places to integrate your storyworld. Pass through the book once, tweaking dialogue to add storyworld phrases, language, and slang. Pass through again and look for storyworld terms that you need to make consistent. For example, in my book *Captives*, people don't "hail" taxis, they "wave" them. But I forget when I'm writing fast, so I catch those types of things in my rewrites.

Edit for consistency in your magic, weather, way-of-life, and any other storyworld details. When working in bits of history, be choosy. It's not necessary to give the reader everything. History can be delivered to the reader in creative ways. One character can tell others a story. A character could find a book of history. Rituals could be performed in religion or for holidays that are based on historical events. Traditions can be based on history, whether it be types of foods, ways of naming children, ceremonies for promoting soldiers, or how the furniture is arranged in a house. Superstitions come from history too. As do cautionary tales or things parents might warn their children about like, "Beware of glowing rocks in the bottom of a lake."

The more times you can re-read your story and tweak and add, the better you'll be able to integrate your storyworld.

PROLOGUES ARE ALLOWED

Prologues have become cliché. If you feel like it's the best way to tell the story, go ahead and use a prologue, but remember two things. First, beware of the cliché prologues that tell an ancient history or leave a baby on a doorstep. If you do this, you need to make yours different and unique, because it's been overdone. Second, make sure the prologue accomplishes something that the rest of the story cannot. If you could delete the prologue and have the exact same story, you probably should get rid of it altogether.

EXTRAS

Using extras in the front, middle, or back of your book can provide the reader with information he can refer to when he has need. Extras are maps, lists of characters, glossaries, charts, and any other documents that might hold a reader's interest. Most of the time these types of things go in the back of the book, so as not to distract the reader from the story or overwhelm him with information.

Robert Jordan's *The Eye of the World* has a glossary in the back that is filled with definitions of terms used in the story. Brandon Sanderson's *Mistborn* has a reference for his magic Allomancy. And in his book, *The Rithmatist,* he has instructional drawings at the start of every chapter that let the reader see how Rithmatics works. In Steven Erikson's *Gardens of the Moon*, he includes a four-page "Dramatis Personae" cast list. I always appreciate a cast list in epic fantasy novels since there are so many characters.

As you're rewriting, think about what information you might include in a list that could be a handy reference for your readers.

DON'T USE EVERYTHING

Look at your storyworld information. Take note of what you've already worked in, and make a list of things that still need to be added somewhere. For those things, brainstorm ways that each aspect might tie in with characters, the overall plot, or subplots. But understand that some things might not find a place. And that's okay.

Just because you thought of it, doesn't mean it has to go in your book. Fight the urge to put in every last detail. Part of worldbuilding is for you to get to know your world, so you can get to know your characters, so you can write a believable fantasy or science fiction story. Use what fits naturally and doesn't feel forced. Leave the rest in your file.

16 MY STORYWORLD

Every person has a life story and a storyworld that is uniquely their own. I was born in Michigan. When I was five, we moved to Alaska. I'm the oldest of five, but at the time of our epic move, we numbered three children. Although my dad had been up in Alaska for several months, getting ready for our arrival, nothing could have prepared my mother for what was to come.

Back then, Alaska offered the last homesteads in the United States. For those of you who've read the *Little House on the Prairie* books, Pa and Almanzo took advantage of homesteading to get free land to live on. My father and uncle wanted to do the same.

My uncle did just that, and to this day, he lives on his forty acres of land just off the Donkey Creek Slough at the foot of Mr. Yenlo, a few miles north of Skwentna. There are no roads to get there. You travel by boat in summer, by snow mobile (snow machine) in winter. Small charter planes can also get you to Skwentna or nearby lakes, but you still need to get yourself from there to your own dock.

My mom didn't go for the homestead life. Since she wanted to put me in school, we found some other places to live. Eventually, my dad started his own, unofficial homestead when he bought a piece of property in Houston, Alaska. There he built a house, bit by bit over the years as he could afford the lumber. He did most all of the work himself with me and my mother holding the occasional board.

It wasn't until I was in college that my parents finally had electricity put in on that land. So I grew up in a home without running water, electricity, or indoor plumbing.

That was my storyworld. That was the place I grew up, the place I lived, the place I called home.

As I lived in that home, I became an expert daydreamer. With no access to television and video games, I spent a lot of time outdoors. When it was too cold to go outside or when, in the summer, the sun never seemed to set, I read books. I inhaled them.

But I didn't want to be a writer. I wanted to be a fashion designer. My mom did a lot of shopping at thrift stores, and I remodeled those clothes to make them fit current trends. But I didn't stop there. I searched old boxes of clothing for things to remake. When I did find a piece of fabric, I'd snip, snip, snip at it like Snoopy making a snowflake, then sew it into some kind of outfit.

My mom panicked many times, watching me, just knowing I was going to waste yards of good fabric. Sometimes I did ruin things, but nine times out of ten I succeeded and created something I wore to school and told everyone I made myself.

Good times.

I chased that dream of fashion design all the way to New York City and later Los Angeles. After five years of working as an assistant fashion designer, I was DONE. It was a *The Devil Wears Prada* environment, and I sucked at being a suck up. Plus, I discovered one day while talking with one of the patternmakers, that my natural skills were in patternmaking, not design. All those years remodeling clothing, cutting up yards of fabric, making something out of nothing . . . I had been able to do that because I was a patternmaker. I could see the shapes of each pattern piece in my mind.

I was a natural builder. Just like my dad.

Sadly, I hadn't gone to school to be a patternmaker, and I didn't want to go back. I had chased the fashion dream, found it wanting, and I wanted out. The dream wasn't what I'd hoped it would be. And that was okay. Never have I had that moment in life when I wondered, "What if I had chased that dream?" Because I chased it. And turns out I didn't like it all that much.

So now I was home. All day. I had my first child. Luke and I hung out. Watched a lot of TV. I got into scrapbooking—big time. My son's first baby book is four inches thick and only covers the first nine months of his life! (I don't do anything half way.)

My husband worked full time, and when he came home, he'd say, "How was your day?" And I'd say . . .

"On *Regis and Kelly* they talked about this. And Natalie Portman was on *Sesame Street*! Oh, and on *The View*, those ladies argued about such-and-such. And Oprah was giving away cars on her show. Dr. Phil did a show about tattoos—his assistant has one across his entire back! And—oh! I have to tell you what's happening on *Days of Our Lives*."

Yes, my life had become routine, indeed.

But I'm a doer. I'm a creator. I'm a builder. So I started a wedding gown business. I even had some of my dresses photographed for *Brides* magazine, but that business didn't work out. Then I dubbed myself the Handbag Lady and started sewing purses and selling them at festivals and bazaars. To this day there is a box of handbags in my basement. Want one?

But I was a builder, and I needed to build things. I had to. I was desperate to. Then something amazing happened. I found books again.

As a kid, I read like crazy, but in high school, I got into fashion and played varsity basketball, and in college, I only had time to read my school books. Then after college, I was working ALL THE TIME.

I had forgotten to read for fun.

But one Thanksgiving, my sister-in-law and her son were staying up late because a new *Harry Potter* book was coming out and they wanted to get in line at midnight at Barnes and Noble to get one of the first copies.

I remembered thinking, "What? I mean, who does that? Wait in line for a new book? Weird."

But a few months later, I went to the library and checked out the first *Harry Potter* book. I mean, I just had to know what was so great about this series that people would sleep in line to get the next one.

And then I saw. I experienced that magical storyworld, and I was hooked. J. K. Rowling was a builder. It wasn't long before I began thinking, "I could do this! How hard could it be?"

Very hard, I'm afraid.

But that's how I got started writing. I wanted to build a storyworld as magical as J. K. Rowling did.

But I don't do it the same way she does. And you won't do it the same way I do. Because we each come from a unique storyworld of our own. You've lived a life that no one else has lived. No one can tell a story quite like you can.

IN CLOSING . . .

The point of storytelling is to entertain and immerse your reader in a gripping story. The way you do that is up to you. No writing rule is absolute. No method is ironclad. This book was designed to help you spark new ideas, but ultimately, you have to figure out how to do this on your own.

I wish I could wave my magic wand and make it all clear for you. But you need this journey.

You need the struggle it brings to your writing life.

Because you're in training, and, for storytellers, the training never ends. There will always be new things to learn, new stories to write.

I hope that I've given you a lot to think about. Yet at the same time, I want you to know that every story isn't that epic, Tolkienesque saga. Some stories are much simpler. Some are about a single storyworld concept and nothing more. Like how a Bigfoot story might be about the mythical creature being found in our world. Or what a high school student would do if he could suddenly read minds.

This book is meant to show you all the areas of worldbuilding, but you need to pick and choose the areas you need for each story you write. You won't ever need everything every time.

If you're looking for more support in your writing journey, please visit www.GoTeenWriters.com. We post five days a week in hopes of encouraging, inspiring, and helping young writers like you.

That's why I wrote this book. I know what it's like to feel clueless about building a storyworld and wanted to share what I've learned.

But you have your own world to build. It will be uniquely yours. Don't take shortcuts. Understand that writing isn't easy. It's a lot of work. But if you respect the industry and craft, take the time to practice and learn, you will be able to create stories that people can't put down. That is totally worth it, don't you think?

You can do it!

chapter ... bonus chapter ... bonus

17 WRITING WAR

How do you write an epic battle?

One point of view at a time.

A full-scale battle isn't much different from writing a one-on-one fight scene. If you're writing clear points of view, you can show only one part of the battle at a time, unless you add in extra narrative or are writing from the point of view of someone on a hill who can see the entire battle spread out before him.

But if you're in one person's head, focus on each action as it comes to him. It's how you coordinate all of these actions that will help you show your epic war.

Back when I was working through the edits for *To Darkness Fled* with my super-cool editor Jeff Gerke, he asked me, "Why is this army traipsing through the woods when they don't know what's ahead? They should send out some scouts. And what about the rearguards?"

I was like, "Um ... What's a rearguard?"

Yeah, I know.

But his question made me realize that I knew nothing about armies or wars. So I had to do some serious research. Turns out armies move slowly, and they don't just wander around, hoping to stumble upon their enemy. (Many of you are saying, "Duh, Jill." But we all have our strengths, and military tactics was not one of mine.)

Commanders send scouts ahead to see where the enemy is and check the lay of the land. This helps the commander decide where to move his group of several hundred—or thousand—soldiers.

Even now, I'm far from an expert, but you don't need to be an expert to tell a fun story. You don't have to learn everything. You just need to learn enough to make your story work.

I did learn the basic layout of an army as it travels and what each part does. I made this little diagram to show you:

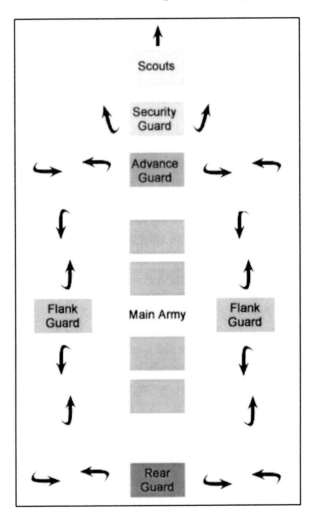

What position your character holds will determine where he travels in such a processional march. Here are the vital areas:

Scouts – These guys ride ahead to locate the enemy. As they do, they consider the terrain to determine the best route for the army to take, whether on foot or if vehicles are involved. Engineers might help scouts decide how to bypass major obstacles.

Security Guard – These guys operate two to six miles in front of the advance guard. Once they find the enemy, the security guard keeps watch on them.

Advance Guard or Vanguard – These soldiers stay one to two miles ahead of the main army to protect it from surprise and to provide cover if a battle starts.

Main Army – This is the biggest part of the army. Each unit should know the situation at all times.

Flank Guard – These fellows operate between the rear of the advance guard and the front of the rear guard to protect the sides of the main army. The flank guard is responsible for reconnaissance along the main army to make sure the enemy doesn't attack from the sides. Flank guards also help with communication between the advance guard and the main army.

Rear Guard – These soldiers operate along the back of the main army and the flank guards. The rear guard must make sure no one sneaks up on the army from the back.

Commander – The commander positions himself in the main army so he can receive information, see the ground, and plan ahead for the deployment of troops. After the enemy is located, the commander should be far enough forward to influence the battle but not so far forward that he loses control of his troops.

But that's only for armies on the move. The layout from an actual battle looks different.

During those same edits, Jeff recommended a book that I found intriguing. It's out of print, but I was able to find a used copy. It's called *Battles of the Medieval World 1000 – 1500*. It goes into detail about many historical battles and includes tactical illustrations of each. Just looking at them sparked ideas for my story.

Here is an illustration I made that shows the layout of the two sides in the Battle of Hastings.

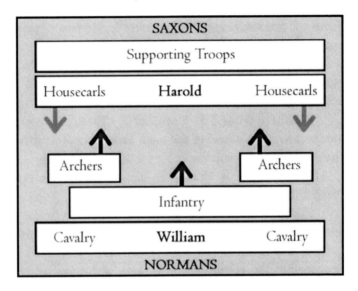

WHAT DO YOU HAVE?

If you're going to write a battle, you need to know some things about each side:

- The layout/formation of each army.
- The terrain.
- Where your main characters are located.
- Roughly how many troops are on both sides.
- The health and well-being of each army.
- The overall scheme of what's happening and why.
- What will happen in the end.
- What types of assets each side has: infantry, cavalry, archers, other weapons like pikes or maces, artillery, magic,

vehicles, beasts, and tactics unique to each side.

Knowing these things should give you enough information to brainstorm different events to help you reach that end result.

As always, you don't have to tell the reader everything. If you're writing from one point of view at a time, you only need to show the reader what's happening with that character's part of the battle.

If you have multiple points of view, you can place your characters in a way that lets the reader know what's going on where. Tolkien did this in *The Return of the King*. We move from scene to scene from Aragorn, Legolas, and Gimli as they recruit the Army of the Dead; to Eowyn and Merry as they fight the Witch King at the battle of Pelennor Fields; and to Gandalf and Pippin as they save Faramir from Denethor's pyre.

So think through your plot and what needs to happen. How you coordinate all the little fight scenes will show your great war.

In my battle research, I came upon a wonderful online resource for coming up with scenes for battles. It's called *The Art of Battle: Animated Battle Maps*. You can watch or download narrated Powerpoint presentations and watch YouTube animations of dozens of historical battles in great detail. Visit their website to see a list of battles at www.theartofbattle.com, or check out their YouTube channel: TheArtofBattle.

In watching some of their battle animations, I picked up some great ideas: War elephants might be cool, but they could rampage at the sight of fire. A storm could come, pouring rain over both armies and making the ground muddy and slippery. An army that wades through a river might be miserably cold, hindering their performance. A confident army that gets drunk the night before a battle makes an easy foe to defeat.

History is filled with great stuff that we can use.

DRAW YOUR OWN BATTLE PLAN

I'm a visual learner. So I sketched a layout for a battle I needed to write for my novel *From Darkness Won*, and it helped me see the terrain, and the general layout and size of each army.

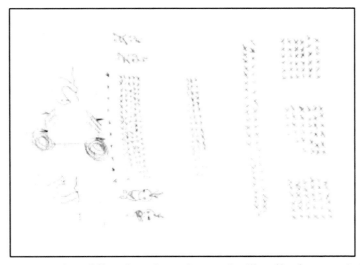

Because I'm addicted to Photoshop and still suffer from periodic relapses of Storyworld Builder's Disease, I recreated the battle in color. Try sketching out your battles. You might find it to be a helpful exercise.

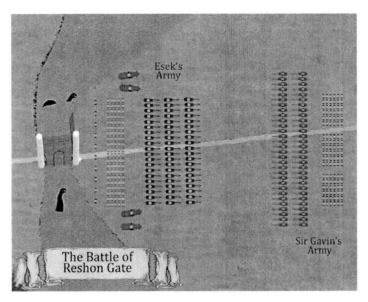

THE WIZARDS' DUEL

What makes a magical battle different from a regular fight? The magic, of course. Everything else about writing a fight scene stays the same. The reader needs to know the motivations for why these people are fighting, where they are, and their skill levels.

So, why *are* they fighting? "The bad guy drew a sword" or "There's a war on" aren't good enough answers. Every character in your book should have a goal, and you, the author, should have a reason for including this particular fight in your story. It must have a purpose. It must make sense. And it must move the story forward. The stakes must justify the action.

Now, even if your hero doesn't know why the other person is picking a fight, you still need to know. And it should come out at some point in the story.

Keep in mind your overall plot. Is this the best time for this fight? You want to slowly build the tension over the course of your book, ratcheting it up to your ending climax. So save your biggest throwdown for near the end of the book or at least near the end of a major development.

My editor, Jeff Gerke, taught me an invaluable tool called Plant and Payoff. He says, "The plant is when you let the reader know that something exists, that something is important, or that a character has an ability or piece of knowledge. The payoff is when you use that thing you've planted."

This works wonders in fight scenes. The reader has to believe that your characters are capable of what you say they do. And if props show up, the reader needs to have seen that vase before it's thrown or knocked over someone's head.

How do you do this? Simply plan for your action scenes ahead of time and plant clues for the reader. If your hero is an expert at your magic, say so early on. Have him practicing with some colleagues or using his ability around the house. If your heroine is good with a bow, let's see her hunting before she's picking off the enemy as they ride horses over a hill.

The goal is to avoid the whole "he's never shot a gun before but picks it up like he's been shooting all his life" thing. Writing conveniently skilled characters is a good way to break the suspension of disbelief and lose your reader. Allow your characters that human trait of failure. Maybe your hero is great at magic, but his enemy has a knife, and his tutor hasn't covered using magic against a blade yet.

Try to choose one of three levels for each character who might get into a fight in your story.

1. Your character knows how to fight and you've shown us early on that he is skilled.

2. Your character is learning to fight, so he will likely lose or get hurt a few times since he isn't very good yet.

3. Your character knows nothing about fighting and gets the tar beat out of him. Ouch.

Just don't fall victim to writing the cliché fighter who's amazing without having had to learn first.

As your characters enter the scene of the pending battle, set the stage with a description that mentions that vase or rock or whatever item(s) your characters might pick up and throw, trip over, or use as an impromptu weapon.

Also, when you choose a setting for the fight, consider an odd locale: a kitchen, a bathroom, a church, a wedding. Something that adds interest, fright, or humor to the scene without being cliché.

Doing these things will help you write awesome fight scenes.

EXTRAS

SOLAR SYSTEM WORKSHEET

Use this worksheet to design a solar system for your story.
Download the full-sized chart at: www.jillwilliamson.com/teenage-authors/helps.

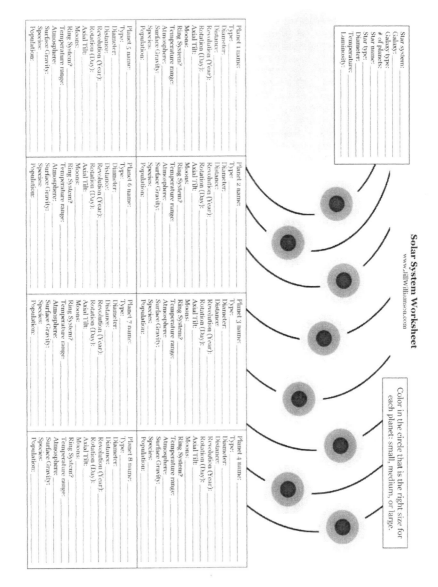

Star system:
Galaxy:
Galaxy type:
# of planets:
Star name:
Star type:
Diameter:
Temperature:
Luminosity:

Planet 1 name:
Type:
Diameter:
Distance:
Revolution (Year):
Rotation (Day):
Axial Tilt:
Moons:
Ring System?
Temperature range:
Atmosphere:
Surface Gravity:
Species:
Population:

Planet 2 name:
Type:
Diameter:
Distance:
Revolution (Year):
Rotation (Day):
Axial Tilt:
Moons:
Ring System?
Temperature range:
Atmosphere:
Surface Gravity:
Species:
Population:

Planet 3 name:
Type:
Diameter:
Distance:
Revolution (Year):
Rotation (Day):
Axial Tilt:
Moons:
Ring System?
Temperature range:
Atmosphere:
Surface Gravity:
Species:
Population:

Planet 4 name:
Type:
Diameter:
Distance:
Revolution (Year):
Rotation (Day):
Axial Tilt:
Moons:
Ring System?
Temperature range:
Atmosphere:
Surface Gravity:
Species:
Population:

Planet 5 name:
Type:
Diameter:
Distance:
Revolution (Year):
Rotation (Day):
Axial Tilt:
Moons:
Ring System?
Temperature range:
Atmosphere:
Surface Gravity:
Species:
Population:

Planet 6 name:
Type:
Diameter:
Distance:
Revolution (Year):
Rotation (Day):
Axial Tilt:
Moons:
Ring System?
Temperature range:
Atmosphere:
Surface Gravity:
Species:
Population:

Planet 7 name:
Type:
Diameter:
Distance:
Revolution (Year):
Rotation (Day):
Axial Tilt:
Moons:
Ring System?
Temperature range:
Atmosphere:
Surface Gravity:
Species:
Population:

Planet 8 name:
Type:
Diameter:
Distance:
Revolution (Year):
Rotation (Day):
Axial Tilt:
Moons:
Ring System?
Temperature range:
Atmosphere:
Surface Gravity:
Species:
Population:

Solar System Worksheet
www.jillwilliamson.com

Color in the circle that is the right size for each planet: small, medium, or large.

CIVILIZATION WORKSHEET

Use this worksheet to design a civilization for your story. Download the full-sized chart at: www.jillwilliamson.com/teenage-authors/helps.

Civilization Worksheet
www.JillWilliamson.com

Civilization
Nation(s): _____ Population: _____
Capital/Ruling City: _____
Other key cities: _____
Type of government: _____ Leader: _____
Taxation: _____
Type of military: _____
Military tactics: _____
Law enforcement: _____
Economic model: _____
Exchange: _____

People
Race/ethnicity/species: _____
Physical features: _____
Mental features: _____
Magical abilities: _____
Family structure: _____ Language: _____
Common sayings/slang: _____
Religion type: _____
Worship style: _____
Education: _____
Way of life: _____
Unique customs: _____
Clothing: _____
What do they eat? _____
Recreation/entertainment: _____
Welfare of general population: _____
Strengths of the people: _____
Fears of the people: _____
Basic nature of the people: _____
Types of jobs: _____

Land
Climate: _____ Weather: _____
Terrain: _____
Landmarks: _____
What it feels like/smells like: _____
Animal life: _____
Plant life: _____
Natural resources: _____
Fuel: _____
Agriculture: _____
Industry: _____
Manufacturing: _____
Types of housing: _____

Technology
Equivalent time period/age: _____
Communication: _____
Medicine: _____
Vehicles: _____
Weapons: _____
Tools: _____

History
Where the city came from: _____
Founders: _____
Wars: _____
Important historical events: _____

MAGIC WORKSHEET

Use this worksheet to design a magic system for your story. Download the full-sized chart at: www.jillwilliamson.com/teenage-authors/helps.

Magic Worksheet
www.JillWilliamson.com

What is the magic? _____

Visual effects? _____

Physical effects? _____

Side effects? _____

Sounds? _____
Where did it come from? _____

Rules: _____

Limitations: _____

Levels of ability: _____

Impact on people: _____

Impact on animals: _____

Impact on the environment: _____

Impact on society: _____

Impact on the economy: _____

Magical symbols:

STORY PLOTTING CHARTS

These plot charts can help in the early stages of planning your book or during rewrites to help you see what's missing. Download the full-sized charts at: www.jillwilliamson.com/teenage-authors/helps.

Scene Plotting Chart

STORY TITLE:
Beginning:
Inciting Incident:
Second Thoughts:
Climax of act 1:
Obstacle:
Obstacle:
Midpoint twist:
Obstacle:
Disaster:
Crisis:
Climax of act 2:
Climax of act 3:
Obstacles:
Denouement:
End:

Scene Plotting Chart for Two Points of View

_____'s POINT OF VIEW	_____'s POINT OF VIEW
Beginning:	Beginning:
Inciting Incident:	Inciting Incident:
Second Thoughts:	Second Thoughts:
Climax of act 1:	Climax of act 1:
Obstacle:	Obstacle:
Obstacle:	Obstacle:
Midpoint twist:	Midpoint twist:
Obstacle:	Obstacle:
Disaster:	Disaster:
Crisis:	Crisis:
Climax of act 2:	Climax of act 2:
Climax of act 3:	Climax of act 3:
Obstacles:	Obstacles:
Denouement:	Denouement:
End:	End:

CHARACTER WORKSHEET

This worksheet is a big help to me as I create characters. I fill out one of these for all my main characters and some of my important minor characters too. You can download the full-sized chart at: www.jillwilliamson.com/teenage-authors/helps.

Character Worksheet

Name:	Famous counterpart:
Age:	One-word descriptor:
Myers/Briggs personality type:	Love language:
Appearance (Tags):	
Titles:	
Day-to-day goal:	
Story goal (external):	
Story goal threatened by:	
Push/pull that makes him act:	
Second goal:	
How it conflicts w/first goal:	
Goal he lives by (internal):	
Emotional life goal:	
How emotional goal shows in behavior:	
They most value? (take it away):	
Willing to die for:	
Greatest dream:	
Noble cause:	
Greatest fear (make it happen):	
Personality descriptors:	
Methods of action:	
Methods of evaluation:	
Skills:	
Flaws:	
Traits/quirks:	
Hobbies:	

EXTRA CONFLICT AND GROWTH

Story change he must face:	
How can I make life worse?	
What can I threaten?	
What else can I take away?	
6 Things that need fixing:	
1.	4.
2.	5.
3.	6.

CHARACTER INTERACTIONS

Protagonist:	Antagonist:
Guardian:	Contagonist:
Reason:	Emotion:
Sidekick:	Skeptic:

PAST

Happiest moment:	
Dark moment:	
Lie they believe:	
Mantra they live by:	

www.jillwilliamson.com

129

CREATURE WORKSHEET

Use this worksheet to design a creature for your story. You can download the full-sized chart at: www.jillwilliamson.com/teenage-authors/helps.

Creature Worksheet
www.JillWilliamson.com

Plot purpose (circle one)

    pet   messenger   transportation   labor   warrior   predator   guard   poisonous   diseased

    wild   domestic   livestock   friend   character   production (wool or other)   source of magic

Other: _____

Looks like: _____
_____

Emotion animal evokes in humans: _____
_____

Unique characteristics: _____
_____

Habitat: _____
_____

Home: _____
_____

Sleep patterns: _____
_____

What it eats: _____
_____

How does it get food? _____
_____

Defense mechanisms: _____
_____

Mating rituals: _____
_____

Sketch your animal here:

A HISTORY OF ER'RETS
FROM THE *BLOOD OF KINGS* TRILOGY

Almost six hundred years ago, the first man to set foot in the wilds of Er'Rets was Kinsman explorer King Echad Hadar. Arman, the one-god, called Echad to cross the great sea in search of a new land. Upon arriving in Er'Rets, the one-god bestowed a special gift upon King Echad and his descendants: the gift of omniscience.

This ability was in no way as strong as Arman's omniscience, but the power enabled King Echad to know the hearts of his people in a special way.

King Echad landed at the southernmost tip of Er'Rets. There he built a small manor with a tower to watch the sea. He named the manor Er'Rets' Point, because Er'Rets meant "land" in the Kinsman old language. In time, Er'Rets would become the name of the entire continent.

In the land surrounding his new manor, King Echad found beasts, birds, and fish that he'd never seen before, but he found no people. Yet with his omniscient ability, he sensed other life existed on Er'Rets and wanted to find it. He left a small group of men to guard the manor and traveled north, searching for signs of life.

He sensed people to the north and set out around the mountains that separated the southern grasslands from what mysteries lay beyond. Before he reached the mountains, however, King Echad discovered a huge lake with waters like glass. He found the area so breathtaking, he could go no farther. He commissioned a second manor, this one of even greater magnitude, to be built in the center of the great lake. There it would be nearly impossible to penetrate.

During the construction, Echad took a small party north to explore beyond the snowy peaks. They soon entered a forest with trees as high as small mountains. Here Echad discovered the first life in this new land that wasn't beast, bird, or fish. He discovered giants.

Thankfully, the giants were peaceful. Although they did not speak the same language, the two groups found ways to communicate. The giants had lived in this land for only a short time, having come from the east. They had no interest in traveling beyond the forest where they'd made their home. King Echad remained with the giants for a few weeks before continuing his journey. He stayed his course north, following his sense that more people lived there.

Echad passed through a barren swampland. Farther north he crossed orchards and wild fields thick with fox, rabbits, and deer. He approached another mountain chain and traveled to the east of it. He discovered vineyards ripe with plump grapes but sensed no people nearby. He followed a river west into the mountains, and after a week, exited on the western side of the land. There he found another forest, smaller than the one the giants lived in, but swarming with a pale race of humans. This people, who called themselves Poroo, lived quite savagely. Although the Poroo did not attack, Echad sensed their hostility, so he turned south. Before long he came to a sea. It did not seem like he should have traveled the whole land yet, so he followed the shore inland until he came to familiar swampland. He crossed back into the giant's forest, then traveled west, to see how far he could go.

The forest gave way to a dry, barren land, and eventually a desert. A pack of rabid wolves attacked, and Echad lost nine of his men before killing the wolves. He continued west until he reached the sea, then followed the coastline south, hoping to return to Er'Rets' Point. As he rounded the mountains, he met a third people. They spoke a similar form of his language, although he had never seen men with such olive-toned skin. These people called themselves Chuma and claimed to have come from the west. They called their city Jaelport. It was a richly decorated castle on the coast of a peninsula. The Chuma were hospitable, but practiced sorcery, which greatly disturbed King Echad, so he decided to continue on. The Chuma were kind enough to ferry King Echad and his men across an inlet, which likely saved them three day's journey.

Great billowing smoke on the horizon alluded to more life ahead. The king and three of his closest men went closer to see what burned. From a distance, they witnessed a barbaric tribe of people. Since their numbers were limited after the wolf attack, the king chose to bypass these barbarians. Farther south they encountered another olive skinned-city. These people lived more simply than the Chuma of Jaelport. Their magic also made King Echad uncomfortable, so he continued south along the coast until he saw the tower of Er'Rets' Point.

King Echad returned to the great lake to check the progress of his fortress. Having found no place more beautiful in all Er'Rets, he decided to live there. He named the castle Armonguard, for Arman would always be its guardian and he wanted the castle to be a tribute to his creator and a reminder to his descendants.

As the years went on, many kings ruled at Armonguard. Scores of wars were fought and won. King Echad Hadar's descendants eventually stretched out across the land, building manors and cities. Over time the kings grew further from Arman's ways, abusing their omniscient abilities, which they now called bloodvoicing, since the ability passed down through the blood of King Echad's descendants. As a result, Arman gifted the people less and less.

During the reign of Silmal Hadar II, two hundred and forty years ago, the gray-skinned Otherlings from the north started a war, which later became known as The Great War. Eventually the Chuma, Poroo, and giants became involved as well. A strange illness came upon King Silmal II, leaving him bedridden. His son, Willham I, secured his father at the refuge fortress of Noiz, then took charge of defending Armonguard.

Arman sent his son to Er'Rets in Kinsman form to teach truth to the people, which even King Silmal II had begun to forget. As Câan fought for truth, then sacrificed himself to save his people, most did not see what he'd accomplished. They deemed the Son God a weak warrior and chose to continue worshiping false gods. Er'Rets fell further into an abyss of evil and selfishness. Over the years, a small group of Câan followers gathered, inducting into their ranks the young Prince Axel Hadar. When Axel became king, he brought with him an obedience to Arman, which had been absent from the House of Hadar for nearly one hundred years. He proclaimed Arman the One God. Many dukes and lords found the young king's beliefs folly, and some took it as treason to their way of life. A plot developed among King Axel's enemies. The next spring, as the king passed through Allowntown on his way to meet with Duke Amal of Carmine, his procession was attacked. The king and queen were murdered, and their three-year-old son, Gidon, vanished.

Instantly, a great Darkness stretched over the land of Er'Rets, starting in the west and settling above a tree in Allowntown, under which the king and queen had been murdered. Many thought the gods were cursing the people for the death of the king. The remnant of Câan, called The Way, believed evil had become too great in Er'Rets. If the people didn't turn back to Arman and give up their wickedness, Darkness might continue to grow until it covered all the land.

For months Kingsguard soldiers searched for the young prince but could not find him. They had given up hope when a young man called Luas Nathak arrived in Mahanaim with the boy, wanting to return him to the Council of Seven. Luas claimed he found the prince child wandering the land near his home and only knew he was royalty because of the signet ring he wore on a chain around his neck.

The Council voted that Luas be knighted for his heroism. The prince was sent to his uncle, Prince Oren Hadar, to be raised, but for reasons unknown, Prince Oren refused him. Sir Luas volunteered to raise the child, having grown close to the boy during their time together. The Council declared Sir Luas Nathak warden for Prince Gidon Hadar until he came of age. Funds were given to make Sir Luas's home more suitable for a prince, thus Sitna Manor was built.

Without a king, the Council of Seven governed Er'Rets and would continue to do so until Prince Gidon came of age. Having declared King Axel's Kingsguard incompetent, the Council inducted a New Kingsguard to protect the prince. Dissenters began to sprout up all over the land, weakening the Council's power and turning the people against each other and the young prince before he even had a chance to rule.

Time has passed, and now the prince has reached his sixteenth year. After his coming of age celebration and tournament, he will be presented to the Council of Seven to claim the throne that is rightfully his.

SAMPLE MAPS

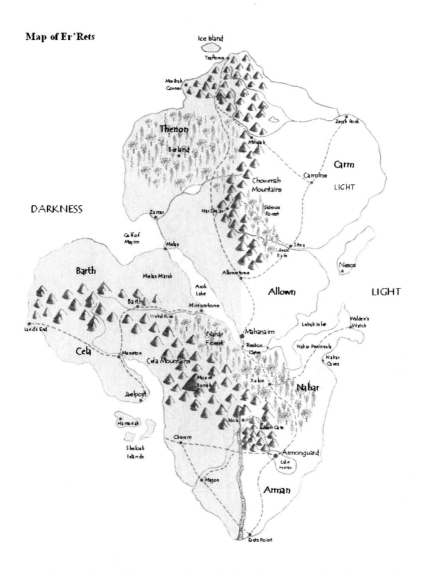

Map of Er'Rets

To explore this map and read the short narratives I wrote for each location during my Blood of Kings pre-writing, visit: www.jillwilliamson.com/explore-errets.

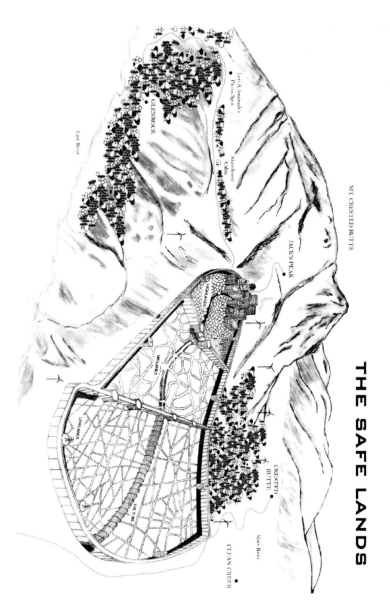

This is a map of the Safe Lands from my teen dystopian books
Captives, Outcasts, and *Rebels*.

This is a map for a series called *The Shardlands* which I started but have yet to finish. I loved making this map. I need to get back to this world . . . soon.

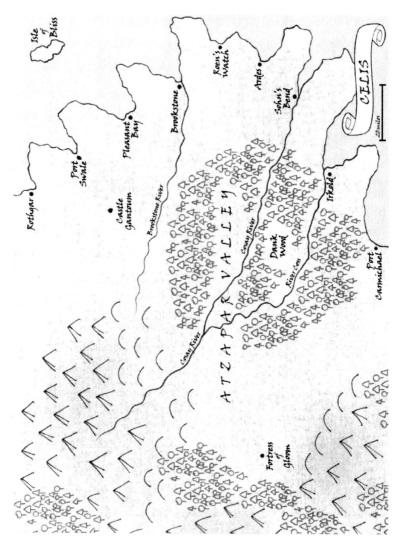

This is a map of Celis that I made for the story *But Who Would Be Dumb Enough to Even Try It?* in which several authors took turns writing a story one chapter at a time. Learn more about the project here: www.enclavepublishing.com/books/dumb-enough-even-try.

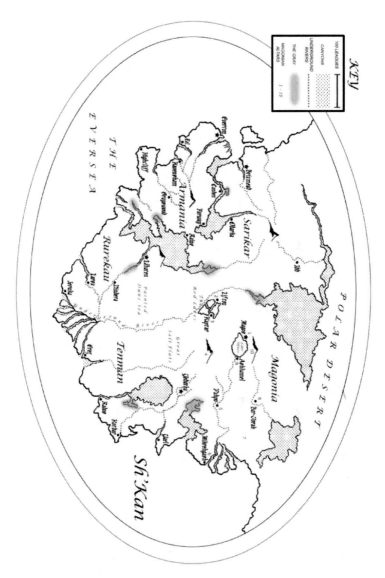

This is a map from my *Kinsman* series, though it has already changed from what you see here. By the time the book is out, you might not recognize it. My biggest mistake was that this land is south of the equator, so my polar desert should be on the bottom, not the top. Such is the life of a map when you make it before you write the book. It changes as you write. And it changes again when you rewrite.

ANSWERS TO SLANG FROM CHAPTER 11

zark – An expletive from the novel *The Hitchhiker's Guide to the Galaxy* by Douglas Adams.

sweet mother of Artemis – A mild oath or an expression of surprise from the *Battlestar Galactica* television series.

son of a hamster – A curse from the film *Get Smart*.

smoke you – A curse from the film *The Fifth Element*.

oh, my prophetic soul – An expression exclaimed by the Fourth Doctor in the *Doctor Who* television episode "The Horns of Nimon."

sleemo – A derogatory Huttese term from the film *Star Wars Episode I: The Phantom Menace*.

mudblood – A derogatory term for a person of mixed Wizarding and Muggle, or non-magical, ancestry from J. K. Rowling's *Harry Potter* novels.

bit brain – A derogatory term that means idiot from the film *Tron*.

cowpog – A derogatory Gnommish term for "idiot" from the novel *Artemis Fowl* by Eoin Colfer.

Shattering glass! – A euphemism used by Bastille in the *Alcatraz* series by Brandon Sanderson.

shiitake mushrooms – An expletive from the film *Spy Kids*.

frak – An expletive from the *Battlestar Galactica* television series.

WORD LIST FOR NAMING FANTASY PLACES

acorn	blossom	cloud
acres	blue	cold
alcove	bluff	cool
amber	bone	corn
anchor	bottom	corner
angel's	branch	cottage
apple	breath	cotton
arbor	bridge	court
ash	bright	cove
auburn	broad	cow
autumn	brook	cozy
axe	brush	creek
balm	bulb	crest
bane	burning	crimson
bank	bush	crooked
barn	butte	crow
bay	butterfly	crystal
bayou	butternut	cut
beacon	cabbage	daisy
beam	cactus	dale
bean	calm	dawn
bear	canyon	day
beaver	castle	death
bend	cat	deer
bent	cave	dell
berry	cherry	devil's
big	chestnut	dew
birch	cider	diamond
bird	cinder	dog
black	circle	dove
blood	claw	dust
bloom	clear	ear

east	glade	isle
easy	glen	ivory
ebony	glove	ivy
echo	goat	jagged
edge	God's	jetty
elder	gold	jewel
elk	goose	journey
elm	grand	knoll
embers	grass	lace
emerald	green	lady's
estate	grove	lagoon
eye	hair	lake
falcon	happy	lamb
fallen	harbor	landing
falls	harvest	lane
fang	haven	lantern
farms	hawk	lazy
fat	hay	leaf
father	hazy	ledge
fawn	heather	leg
feather	heights	lemon
fern	herb	lichen
field	hickory	lily
finger	hidden	little
fir	high	loft
fire	highlands	log
flats	hill	lone
flower	hollow	lonely
foggy	holly	long
foot	honey	lord's
forest	horn	lost
fox	horse	lump
fur	house	manor
gardens	hush	mantle
gate	iron	maple
gentle	island	meadow

merry	pine	sandy
mews	pioneer	saunter
middle	place	sea
mill	pleasant	seed
mint	pod	shade
misty	point	shadow
moon	poison	shady
mother	pond	shoal
mountain	pony	shrug
mouth	poplar	side
mud	prairie	silent
mule	pretty	silver
nectar	pumpkin	skull
nest	quail	sky
nettle	quaint	sleepy
niche	quaking	small
night	quay	snake
noble	quiet	snare
nook	rabbit	south
north	race	sparrow
nose	ramble	spike
nut	red	spring
oak	ridge	spruce
old	rise	square
orange	river	squirrel
orchard	road	star
pace	robin	stead
paint	rock	still
panda	rocky	stone
park	root	street
pass	rose	stroll
path	rough	strong
peach	round	summit
pearl	row	sun
pebble	run	swale
pied	rustic	swan
pike	sand	sweet

tawny	trek	wander
tender	turn	wart
terrace	twilight	water
thistle	twin	way
thorn	twist	weed
thunder	umber	west
timber	vale	wheat
toad	valley	white
toe	velvet	wild
tongue	view	willow
top	villa	windy
trace	vine	wood
trail	vista	yew
treasure	wagon	zephyr
tree	walnut	

WORD LIST FOR NAMING SCIENCE FICTION PLACES

absorption	atmosphere	comet
acceleration	atomic	compiler
accumulation	attack	composition
acid	automation	compound
acidic	avatar	compression
adaptation	axis	condensation
affect	bacteria	conduction
agrarian	balance	cone
airborne	base	conservation
alignment	behavior	constant
allele	biome	constellation
alliance	biosphere	construct
alluvium	black hole	constructor
alteration	blast	convention
alveoli	blaster	cool
amphibian	breach	core
amplitude	buoyancy	cosmic
analysis	calcium	crater
animation	capacity	crystal
anodize	capillary	culture
anomaly	carapace	cyber
anti	catalyst	cybernetic
antigen	cell	cyborg
apparatus	centrifugal	cycle
application	change	cytoplasm
aquatic	chemical	dark
arboreal	chromosome	data
assembler	chronic	death
assessment	classification	decay
asteroid	climate	decibel
astro-	clone	density
astrogate	cloud	deposit

depth	examination	gestalt
developmental	exo-	gestation
digestible	expansion	global
dilute	experimental	gravitational
dimension	exploration	gravity
directional	explosion	gun
discovery	exposure	habitat
disease	extreme	heat
displacement	fault	holographic
dissection	fauna	host
dissolution	feldspar	human
dissolve	fight	hydrogen
distance	fire	hyper
disturbance	fission	hyperspace
drive	fissure	hypothesis
earth	flora	identification
eclipse	force	illuminator
ecological	force field	illusion
ecosystem	forecast	imaginary
effect	formations	impact
electrical	frequency	implant
electron	friction	indigenous
elemental	FTL (faster than	inertia
elevation	light)	instrument
embryonic	functional	intelligence
endangered	fundamental	interaction
energy	fusion	interplanetary
environmental	galactic	interpreter
enzyme	galaxy	inverse
equilibrium	gamma	ions
erosion	gamma-ray	isotope
escape	gas	kinetic
evaporation	gastric	laser
event	generation	latitude
evidence	geothermal	law
evolutionary	germination	lethal

life
lift
light
luminous
lunar
machine
manifold
mantle
mass
matter
mechanical
meteor
microbe
mineral
modulator
module
moisture
molecule
moon
motion
movement
mutation
nanite
nano
nanobot
navigation
needle
neutron
nocturnal
nuclear
observation
orbit
organ
organism
osmosis
oxygen
panel

particle
percolator
perma-
phenomena
physical
planet
planetary
plasma
pod
polar
pollination
polymer
population
port
positronic
precipitation
precognitive
preservation
pressure
primary
probe
process
property
protection
proton
quantum
quark
quest
radiation
radioactivity
ratio
ray
reaction
reactor
reagent
reboot
recovery

refraction
region
replicant
replicator
research
resistance
resonator
ripper
robot
safety
sapient
satellite
saturation
scenario
science
scientific
scientist
screen
security
sedentary
seismic
sensors
sensory
sentient
sequence
shield
shift
simulator
situation
solar
soluble
solvent
sonar

sonic	synthesis	universal
sound	synthetic	universe
source	system	vacuum
space	tech	vapor
species	technology	variable
spectrum	tectonic	velocity
speed	temperature	vidscreen
sphere	terrestrial	virtual
stage	theoretical	virus
star	theory	visible
station	thermal	vision
stellar	thermometer	vital
stimulus	thrust	voltage
sub-	time	voyage
subspace	torque	warp
substance	toxin	wave
subterranean	transformation	world
surface	transporter	x-ray
survival	trap	yield
symbiotic	travel	zero-impact
synergy	tube	zone

WORD LIST FOR CURSES AND INSULTS

accursed	cavernous	fecked
addled	chicken	fed
arse	churlish	filth
artless	clawed	flushed
badgered	clobbered	fool
base	clod	fool-born
bashed	clumpish	foul-looking
battered	cockeyed	fried
bawdy	corned	fuddled
befuddled	coward	gassed
bent	coxcomb	giddy
besotted	craven	glutton
big	crude	goatish
biting	crunkered	goosed
bitten	cuckold	greedy
blackened	cur	gutted
blackguard	daisy	guttered
blasted	dank	hag
blathered	degenerate	halfwit
bloated	demon	hammered
blossom	devil	hanging
boiled	dimwitted	hedge-born
bootless	dolt	hinny
bootlicker	donkey	hog-bodied
brain-boiled	dragon	howling
brained	drunken	ill-bred
bride	dull	jack
brute	dunce	jerk
buggering	dung	jolly
buttered	eating	juiced
buzzed	evildoer	knave
cabbaged	fat	lard
canker	feather	lawbreaker

leathered	plucked	surly
lecher	plumpish	swacked
legless	portly	thickset
liar	profligate	tickle-brained
libertine	purveyor	tipsy
lit	quailing	toad-spotted
little	rake	toasted
livered	rascal	trickster
looped	ratsbane	troll
louse	ratty	tweaked
lousy	reeky	twisted
low-born	reprobate	twit
lumpish	roaring	twizzled
maggot	roguish	ugly
mangled	rotund	unclean
mare	rough-hewn	vexing
mashed	ruined	vile
maudlin	rump	villain
merry	ruttish	vulgar
mewing	saucy	wagtail
milksop	scattered	wallowing
minced	scoundrel	wantwit
miscreant	scullion	warped
mottled	shrew	wasted
muddled	simpleton	wastrel
mule	snouted	wayward
nighthawk	sodden	wench
no-good	sour-faced	whelp
nut	spongy	whey-faced
oaf	squiffy	wicked
odiferous	squished	wind-breaking
old	steam-pigged	witch
paunchy	stewed	witted
peddler	stiff	wrecked
piggish	stinking	wretch
pillock	strumpet	yeasty

EXAMPLES OF DOGGEREL

Both of these come from my *Blood of Kings* trilogy. The first is a song a girl sung to my hero in an effort to court him. The second is a chorus that people began to sing about the new king (warning: spoilers). For fun, I put both to music, though I'm not a professional. You can listen to them here: www.jillwilliamson.com/free-downloads-2

View Not My Face

View not my face, I am undone beside you.
The beating of my heart will not cease.
Whilst I am near you, whilst I am near you.

Pity on my heart, from the day I first saw you.
Your pleasing face burns my memories.
Whenever we're apart, whenever we're apart.

Though I am nothing to you, I love you, I do.
How shall I make it known, that I love you?

The Pawn Our King

He grew up here in Sitna Town,
The hand his life was dealt.
He milked the goats and fetched the wood
Or Poril gave him the belt.

The pawn our king, sing merry, merry, merry.
The pawn our servant king.
For he was once the lowest of all strays
And now claims to be king.

Then the Great Whitewolf took him up,
Taught him to use a sword.
He fought quite well, his blade struck true,
And blood from Esek poured.

Remember us, sing merry, merry, merry.
Remember us, O king.
For you were once the lowest of all strays
And now you'll be our king.

WRITING CRAFT TERMS

Backstory: What happened to your characters before your story began.

Conflict: That which causes your character to struggle.

Genre: A category of literature.

Motivation: The reason a character chooses to do something.

Narrative: When the story moves into narration, or telling, to explain what's happening outside a character's point of view.

Plant and Payoff: To set up beforehand any information that will be used in a later scene so that the reader knows something exists before it's used in action in the story. Coined by Jeff Gerke.

Point of view (POV): The character who is acting as narrator and telling the story at that moment.

Progression of belief: A group of events in which a character comes to believe in the impossible.

Scene: A section of a story that represents a single episode or event.

Storyworld: The setting of your story.

Subgenre: A sub-category of literature.

Suspension of disbelief: The reader's willingness to suspend doubt and believe the unbelievable for the sake of enjoyment.

SPECULATIVE FICTION SUBGENRES

Speculative fiction is the supergenre of everything that falls under science fiction and fantasy. It's a term that encompasses all the "weird" fiction genres. Speculative fiction can take place on earth but often takes place in other worlds envisioned by the author.

Subgenres don't really matter to most readers. Within the YA or Adult headings, these books are usually shelved in the same section at your local bookstore. But for authors, knowing your subgenre is important so that you can write to a specific audience and so that you're able to pitch your story to an agent or editor.

Here is a list of popular subgenres. I've done my best to define them simply. There are many more, and for those that I've listed, there's still a lot of crossover between them. See if you can find at least one subgenre for the story you're writing.

Alternate History – Any story that messes with the history of our world. For example: What if Germany won World War II? Harry Turtledove is one of the most prolific writers of the alternate history genre. Scott Westerfeld's *Leviathan* is a middle grade alternate history story.

Apocalyptic fiction – Stories in this subgenre tell tales of the end of the world. This might come from nuclear war, pandemics, the return of Messiah, technology, or general disasters. Some examples are *World War Z* by Max Brooks, the *Left Behind* series by Tim LaHaye and Jerry B. Jenkins, and Stephen King's *The Stand*.

Contemporary fantasy (or modern fantasy) – These are fantasy stories set in our present-day world. Oftentimes the hero discovers a world within our world. The *Harry Potter* and *Percy Jackson* books are two examples of contemporary fantasy stories.

Cyberpunk – These types of stories deal with high-tech cybernetics. They might be stories about artificial intelligence, information technology, virtual reality, hackers, computers, cyborgs, or clones. The stories may take place on a near-future earth, a far-future one, or another planet. Some examples are *The Matrix*, *Blade Runner*, *The Terminator*, and *Cinder* by Marissa Meyer.

Dark Fantasy (or gothic fantasy) – These books are a combination of fantasy and horror. They don't always have clear good and bad guys, and good does not always win. These stories often have a feeling of impending doom or dread. Some dark fantasy takes place in mythical storyworlds. Think *Beowulf*, Anne Rice's *Vampire Chronicles*, Stephen King's *The Dark Tower* series, and *Miss Peregrine's Home for Peculiar Children* by Ransom Riggs.

Dystopian – These are stories that take place in a repressive or controlled futuristic world. Often under the guise of being perfect, the characters are living a real-life nightmare. These are often cautionary tales of where current society might be headed. Suzanne Collins's *The Hunger Games*, Lois Lowry's *The Giver*, James Dashner's *Maze Runner*, Veronica Roth's *Divergent*, and my *Safe Lands* trilogy are all examples.

Epic Fantasy (or high fantasy) – These are stories set in a mythical storyworld that differs in some way from our primary world (earth). These books have a very large cast. They have a huge focus on the detail of the storyworld, and usually, the world is at stake. Magical elements are often included. Examples are Tolkien's *The Lord of the Rings* series, Steven Erikson's *Gardens of the Moon*, Robert Jordan's *Wheel of Time* series, Brandon Sanderson's *The Way of Kings*, and Robin Hobb's *Assassin* stories.

Fairytales – These types of stories typically feature characters from folklore such as: fairies, goblins, elves, trolls, dwarves, witches, sorcerers, and giants. Fairytales usually have magical elements. Most traditional fairytales came from Hans Christian Andersen or the Brothers Grimm. *The Goose Girl* by Shannon Hale is a retelling. *Ella Enchanted* by Gail Carson Levine is an original fairytale.

Hard Science Fiction – These are science fiction stories loaded with, not just science but, accurate science. Arthur Clarke's *2001: A Space Odyssey* is an example of hard science fiction, as is Kim Stanley Robinson's *Mars* series.

Heroic Fantasy – These types of stories follow a smaller cast of sword-wielding heroes as they go on quests to stop evil. These books have lots of action and are shorter than epic fantasy. Robert E.

Howard's *Conan* books are heroic fantasy, as are Joe Abercrombie's *The Blade Itself*, David Gemmel's *Legend*, R. Scott Bakker's *The Prince of Nothing* series, Michael Moorcock's *Elric* novels, and my own *Blood of Kings* trilogy.

Militaristic Science Fiction – These stories deal with war and military storylines. Realistic battles, details about chain of command, and accurate weaponry matters in these books. Think *Ender's Game* by Orson Scott Card, Jack Campbell's *Lost Fleet* series, David Webber's *Honor Harrington* books, and Robert Heinlein's *Starship Troopers*.

Paranormal – These are stories take place in our world but include phenomena outside the range of what's normal here on earth. Paranormal encompasses a broad range of subjects like: vampires, shapeshifters, ghosts, time travel, psychics, telekinesis, aliens, and any kind of cryptids (Big Foot or the Loch Ness Monster). Some paranormal movies are *The Exorcist*, *Ghostbusters*, and *The Sixth Sense*. Most paranormal books cross over into other subgenres like dark fantasy, urban fantasy, or paranormal romance.

Paranormal Romance – These stories have all the elements of a regular paranormal, but the romance is the gist of the plot. Paranormal romance readers are expecting a "Happily ever after" ending, so if that's not what you're writing, it might not be a romance. *Twilight* is a young adult paranormal romance, as are Richelle Mead's *Vampire Academy* novels.

Post-apocalyptic fiction – These stories are set in a civilization after an apocalyptic event, or perhaps years later. Such stories sometimes fall into the dystopian category if new governments have taken control. Jeanne DuPrau's middle grade novel *City of Ember* is a good example of post-apocalyptic fiction, as is Richard Matheson's *I Am Legend*.

Science Fantasy – Books in this category give a scientific realism to things that could not possibly happen. Science fiction is largely based on established scientific theories, while science fantasy is mostly implausible. The *John Carter of Mars* books by Edgar Rice Burroughs and Anne McCaffrey's *Pern* novels are examples of this subgenre. Another example is Stuart Vaughn Stockton's *Starfire*, which is a story about dinosaur people.

Soft Science Fiction – In a true science fiction story, the majority of the action takes place in our world and universe. It may or may not happen in a futuristic setting. Science fiction always deals with the impact of imagined innovations in science or technology and does not violate the laws of nature. Everything is plausible. The reader is drawn into the "what if" of the story by knowing that this scenario could actually happen. Soft science fiction tends to focus more on the social sciences of characters, their emotions, and humanity than it does on hard science. An example of a soft science fiction novel is *The House of the Scorpion* by Nancy Farmer. Dystopian and utopian novels also fall under the soft science fiction umbrella. Think George Orwell's *Nineteen Eighty-Four*.

Space Opera – Space opera stories are set entirely in outer space. They are large-scale, dramatic adventures where the heroes face dastardly villains. Space operas tend to have several elements in common: long journeys in space crafts that have cool names, political unrest, a group of rebels (often our heroes), a massive space port or mothership, bizarre alien life forms, and weapons with cool names.

Star Wars, Battlestar Galactica, Firefly, Frank Herbert's *Dune*, and *A Fire Upon the Deep* by Vernor Vinge are all examples.

Steampunk – These stories sometimes fall into a subgenre of alternate history, though they may be entirely fantasy. They combine elements of science fiction or fantasy and are written in a time period when steam power is still widely used—usually the 19th century. Victorian era Britain is a popular setting, as is a wild west-type world (western steampunk). Fictional machines in steampunk are often inspired by the works of H. G. Wells and Jules Verne. Examples are Maureen McQuerry's *The Peculiars* and Scott Westerfeld's *Leviathan*, which is both alternate history and steampunk.

Superhero Fiction – This is a type of fiction that follows characters with superhuman abilities that come up against dastardly villains trying to take over the world—or maybe just a certain city. These types of stories are inspired by comic books like *Superman, Captain America, The Green Lantern, Batman*, and so on. *Failstate* by John W. Otte is a good example of a superhero fiction novel.

Supernatural – These types of stories remove all elements that fall under fantasy and horror, and embrace supernatural elements that are considered commonplace in the natural world. Things like angels, demons, God, and Satan. Shannon Dittemore's *Angel Eyes* series is great example of the supernatural subgenre. And my Mission League series has supernatural elements as well.

Techno-thriller – These stories combine the genres of thriller, science fiction, and action. They often include spies and/or war and tend to have more technical details than your average thriller. Many science fiction novels fall under this subgenre. A great example is the work of Michael Crichton.

Urban Fantasy (paranormal fantasy) – These are contemporary stories that take place in our world and deal with a dark underworld. They often take place in a city and have mystery plots with the pacing of a thriller. Think *Buffy the Vampire Slayer*, Cassandra Clare's *The Mortal Instruments* series, Jim Butcher's *Dresden Files*, or Carrie Vaughn's *Kitty* novels.

BOOKS I RECOMMEND

FANTASY AND SCIENCE FICTION CREATION

•*How to Write Science Fiction & Fantasy* by Orson Scott Card

RESEARCH

•*Medieval Swordsmanship: Illustrated Methods and Techniques* by John Clements
•*The Time Traveler's Guide to Medieval England* by Ian Mortimer
•*Battles of the Medieval World: 1000 - 1500* by Devries, Dougherty, Dickie, Jestice, and Jorgensen
•*100 Decisive Battles* by Paul K. Davis

GENERAL WRITING CRAFT

•*Go Teen Writers: How to Turn Your First Draft into a Published Book* by Stephanie Morrill and Jill Williamson
•*Self-Editing for Fiction Writers* by Renni Browne and Dave King
•*Writing Fiction for Dummies* by Randy Ingermanson
•*On Writing* by Stephen King
•*Stein on Writing* by Sol Stein
•*Writing the Breakout Novel* by Donald Maass
•*Save the Cat* by Blake Snyder (A book on screenwriting that will teach you a lot about how to tell a story.)

GRAMMAR AND PUNCTUATION

•*The Chicago Manual of Style*
•*The Elements of Style* by Strunk and White

BIBLIOGRAPHY

Bowker, John. *The Oxford Dictionary of World Religions*. Oxford: Oxford University Press, 1997. Print.

Card, Orson Scott. *How to Write Science Fiction & Fantasy*. Cincinnati: Writers Digest Books, 1990. Print.

Demaitre, Luke E. *Medieval Medicine: The Art of Healing, from Head to Toe*. Santa Barbara: Praeger, 2013. Print.

Devries, Kelly, et al. *Battles of the Medieval World: 1000 - 1500*. London: Amber Books, 2006. Print.

Ergil, Kevin, et al. *Ancient Healing: Unlocking the Mysteries of Health and Healing Through the Ages*. Lincolnwood: Publications International, 1997. Print.

Lusco, Andy. Personal interview. 28 July 2014.

Merriam-Webster's Collegiate Dictionary, 11th ed. New York: Merriam-Webster, 2007. Print.

Mortimer, Ian. *The Time Traveler's Guide to Medieval England*. New York: Simon & Schuster, 2008. Print.

Rapkin, Chester. "Urban Planning Theorist." *New York Times* 3 February 2001. Web. 1 August 2014.

Rowling, Marjorie. *Life in Medieval Times*. New York: Penguin Putnam, 1973. Print.

Stross, Randall. "The Birth of Cheap Communication (and Junk Mail)." *New York Times* 20 February 2010. Web. 31 July 2014.

ACKNOWLEDGEMENTS

Thanks to Virginia Frances Sterrett, whose wonderful artwork is now in the public domain, allowing me to use it on my cover.

Thanks to Brooklynne Pereira for modeling for my cover.

Thanks to Andy Lusco for helping me with my government chapter.

Thanks to Amy Bohannan, Melody Bohannan, Griff Charleston, Alexandria K. Mintah, Karina Nora Schink, and Michaella Valkenaar for your keen proofreading eyes.

Thanks to Orson Scott Card, Jeff Gerke, and every other writing instructor I learned from over the years.

Thanks to Stephanie Morrill for letting me blog about writing at www.GoTeenWriters.com.

Thanks to Amanda Luedeke, my agent, who listens to all my random ideas and who graciously supported this project and helped me with the speculative fiction subgenres.

Thanks to my family, who knows more than they ever wanted to know about books and the publishing industry.

Thanks to every teen writer out there. I love that you dream and create stories. Don't ever stop, even when you're not a teen anymore (though you'll always be a teen at heart).

And a big thank you to those of you who've found me online or at writers conferences. I love hearing about your stories. Keep on writing!

Free Jill Williamson S-6-7 ebook Sampler

The ultimate introduction to the writings of Jill Williamson. **Five** chapters each from **six** books and a **seventh** complete short story.

How to get yours:

www.jillwilliamson.com/slcc
available in epub, mobi, and pdf

Come hang out with us!

Contests, encouragement, and community for young writers.

www.GoTeenWriters.com
And join the community of writers on Facebook:
http://www.facebook.com/groups/goteenwriters

And if you're
ready to edit,
check out the
Go Teen Writers
book!

 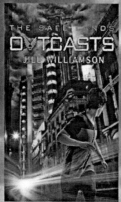 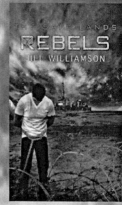

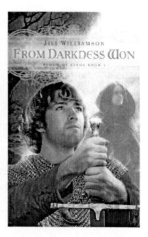

.

waves good-bye